A PARTNER IN THE DYNAMIC OF CREATION

Womanhood in the Teachings of the Lubavitcher Rebbe, Rabbi Menachem M. Schneerson

ב"ה

A PARTNER IN THE DYNAMIC OF CREATION

Womanhood in the Teachings of
the Lubavitcher Rebbe,
Rabbi Menachem M. Schneerson

Edited by Uri Kaploun

Sichos In English
788 Eastern Parkway
Brooklyn, New York 11213

5755 • 1994
הי' תהא שנת נפלאות המשיח

A Partner in the Dynamic of Creation

Published and Copyrighted by
SICHOS IN ENGLISH
788 Eastern Parkway, Brooklyn, N.Y. 11213
Tel. (718) 778-5436

ISBN 1-8814-0011-5

5755 • 1994

Table of Contents

Publisher's Foreword

One day in the 1770s, when the classical Torah under-
pinnings of the fledgling chassidic movement were not
yet widely known, the Alter Rebbe, with self-effacing
dignity, ascended the tall pulpit in the cold synagogue of
Shklov, a major bastion of Lithuanian erudition. As he stood
there, facing the town's scholastic elite, his humorless detrac-
tors sat up straight, ready to assail him zealously with hostile
queries and legalistic objections.

How might one expect an intellectual giant of his caliber
to react? Should he not proceed to analyze and answer their
queries one by one, here resolving a logical paradox, there
supplying a learned source for a problematic postulate?

The Alter Rebbe did none of these. Instead, he quietly
sang a haunting chassidic melody, and in it they heard the
intense yearning of a lofty soul. As its sweet and mellow
warmth stole into their frigid hearts, he elevated his listeners
to an unaccustomed spiritual vantage point. From this new
perspective they were now able to perceive harmony in place
of dissonance, to appreciate brotherliness in place of dissen-
sion, to see the varied facets of the Torah as complementary
hues of a single rainbow, rather than an excuse for sterile
cerebral fisticuffs.

In much the same way, when addressing the sensitive issues confronting Jewish women today, the Rebbe does not

follow the common path of engaging in polemics and apolo-
getics. Instead, by unveiling and illuminating the human and
cosmic repercussions of each of the major *mitzvos* of women,
the Rebbe elevates us to an intellectual and spiritual perspective from which we behold a refreshingly broad world-
picture.

From this perspective, everything is different — womanhood, motherhood, Torah study and *mitzvah* observance.
From this perspective, as she carefully checks the *kashrus* of
the local supermarket's food products, a woman now understands that she is affecting the spiritual and even the physical
well-being of her family. As she lovingly observes the laws of
family purity, she knows that she is not only affecting the
spiritual and physical well-being of her family: she is building
eternity. As she grooms the body and soul of her home on
Friday, she grasps that she is a priestess in G-d's sanctuary,
privileged to treat her family to the experience of *Shabbos*, a
foretaste of the World to Come. And as she discreetly
deploys all her feminine intuition and ingenuity toward
keeping her marriage fresh and loving, she realizes that she is
simultaneously reinvigorating the cosmic marriage bond
between Israel and her Groom.

The proportion of his time that the Rebbe consistently
allocated to promoting the status and interests of women, is
in itself instructive. A few examples: Every year, during the
week before Rosh HaShanah, the Rebbe devoted a major
address to an audience of thousands of women of all ages.[1] At

---

1. On one of those occasions, shortly before Rosh HaShanah 5749, the Rebbe
    proposed that every housewife permanently affix a charity box (popularly
    known by its Yiddish name as a *pushke*) to a prominent spot in her kitchen.
    A little later, on the very eve of Rosh HaShanah, as thousands of women
    filed past the door of his study to receive his blessing with the approach of
    the New Year, the Rebbe reminded many of those who had not yet managed

some time between Lag BaOmer and Shavuos, there was an address in honor of the annual convention of N'shei uBnos Chabad, the Lubavitch Women's Organization which the Rebbe founded in the US in 5713 [1953]. From 5716 [1956] the convention was honored every year by an instructive and inspirational letter in Yiddish and English.[2] Towards the end of the school year there was always an address for the graduating class of Beth Rivkah and for the counselors of the Chabad-Lubavitch summer camps for girls, who were traditionally joined by great numbers of other women and girls. In addition, there was always a letter addressed to the participants of the midwinter convention of N'shei Chabad, held in rotation in various cities throughout the United States, and to the participants of scores of parallel conventions and events held in *Eretz Yisrael*.

Significantly, it was the Rebbe who personally set the tone for the editorial policy of *Di Yiddishe Heim*, the English/Yiddish quarterly of the Lubavitch Women's Organization. On a dozen occasions the Rebbe marked a significant date in the chassidic calendar (such as, in recent years, 22 Shvat, the *yahrzeit* of the *Rebbitzin* Chayah Mushka ע״ה) by handing a newly-published *kuntreis* to each of the women and men present. And countless women throughout the world, like countless men throughout the world, treasure to this day the letters which the Rebbe somehow found time to address to them individually, in response to ideological queries, requests for guidance in their personal or public lives, or requests for enlightenment or intercession.

---

to do this, to turn their homes into "homes of charity" by affixing their box in place before the beginning of the festival that very evening.

2. In 5741 [1981], N'shei uBnos Chabad marked its 25th National Convention by sponsoring a commemorative volume entitled *Letters by the Lubavitcher Rebbe*, which was prepared for publication by Sichos In English and published by Kehot Publication Society.

Throughout those beautiful years during which the Rebbe received individuals and families for private audience (*yechidus*), both women and men in their tens of thousands were privileged to open their hearts to the Rebbe, and leave his presence with renewed strength and direction. In later years, other opportunities were opened to the menfolk — whether of the chassidic community or beyond it — of meeting the Rebbe face to face, soul to soul, for a fleeting but precious moment. And the very same opportunities were made available for the women and girls. During the New Year season, for example, usually on Hoshana Rabbah, the Rebbe personally handed the traditional slice of sweet cake (*lekach*) to vast numbers of women, each of whom heard the Rebbe's voice as he offered them individually his blessings for "a good and sweet year."

Finally, for six crowded years, the unique forum that came to be known throughout the world as simply "dollars" enabled innumerable thousands of men and women from all walks of life and from every corner of the world to be enriched and energized by a brief but unforgettable moment. To each of them the Rebbe handed a dollar to be given to charity and offered his blessings for success in their lifework, often adding an individual comment of direction or encouragement, and sometimes listening and responding to brief requests.[3]

A Partner in the Dynamic of Creation is a thought-provoking collection of ten essays outlining a sampling of the

---

3.   In actual practice, recipients often chose to give away a different dollar bill, together with (in accordance with the Rebbe's request) an additional contribution of their own.

     Dollars were first distributed on 11 Shvat 5746 [1986], and thereafter on a regular basis (on Sundays and on certain other occasions) from 11 Nissan of that year until the day before Monday, 27 Adar I, 5752 [1992].

Rebbe's teachings on subjects of particular interest to women
— social involvement, equal rights, family planning, en-
lightened parenting, women's Torah study and mitzvah observance, and many other topical subjects. The essays are
based on a selection out of the hundreds of talks which the
Rebbe addressed at various times to audiences of women
and/or men in Crown Heights, New York, as adapted over
the years by Rabbi Sholom Ber Hecht, Rabbi Yosef Halevi
Loebenstein and Rabbi Eliyahu Touger. The adaptations as
first published at their respective times by Sichos In English[4]
were reworked, amplified and annotated for the present collection by Uri Kaploun. The project was conceived and nurtured from beginning to end by Rabbi Yonah Avtzon, Direc-
tor of Sichos In English. The Overview was written by Malka
Touger; Yosef Yitzchok Turner gave the book its refreshing
layout and typography; and Avrohom Weg designed the
cover.

"The words of tzaddikim endure forever."[5] Every insight
and every request and every directive of the Rebbe continues
to address us today as it did in years past — if not with the
same intensity as before, then with more. With this in mind,
we at Sichos In English are confident that the insights, requests and directives presented in this work will fall upon
attentive ears and find their sure way into responsive hearts.
And when that happens, every reader who responds by acting
may rest assured that his/her response will bring the Rebbe's

---

4. Adaptations of the above and many other themes which are incorporated in
the above-mentioned ten essays were originally published by Sichos In English as full-length essays in their own right; e.g., "Mazel-Tov: A Blessing for
Mother and Child" (cf. p. 58 below) and "The Shabbos Lights" (cf. p. 82
below).

5. Phrase often quoted by the Rebbe from the Igros Kodesh (Letters) of the
Rebbe Rayatz (e.g., Vol. II, number 470).

lifework one step closer to speedy fruition, with the coming of *Mashiach* in our own days.

Sichos In English

Rosh Chodesh Kislev, 5755

Overview

by
Malka Touger

ONE WOMAN'S THOUGHTS

This overview came to be written shortly after *Gimmel* Tammuz. I found this timing significant, because for the entire year after the *Rebbitzin* Chayah Mushka ע״ה passed away, the Rebbe recalled the verse,[1] — והחי יתן אל לבו "And the living shall take it to heart." Writing this overview thus turned into an opportunity to take to heart the values the Rebbe endeavored to implant within women and the goals which he brought within their sights.

It is also significant that the overview and the essays that follow it are being published in English. In an expanded sense, the concept of translation has a lot to do with the way we relate to the Rebbe's thoughts. The Rebbe's ideas often have to be translated — and not necessarily because of a language barrier. Even when a person understands the Rebbe's words, effort is needed to take his thoughts to heart, and to integrate them into our own thoughts. The Rebbe never intended his thoughts to remain abstract. On the contrary, his thrust has always been directed to applied wisdom, that

---

1. *Koheles* 7:2.

ideals be given expression in our lives. This requires thinking over and thinking out the themes which we have heard from the Rebbe until they become personally relevant.

The very fact that ideas have been taken from the language in which they were initially articulated and transposed into another, represents the first stage in such a process of thinking over and thinking out. The following personal insights and thoughts are offered in this spirit. Obviously, they do not profess to be an authoritative statement on the Rebbe's message to women. Instead, my intent has been to think creatively about these subjects, in the hope that others will be stimulated to discover and be enriched by more of the colors that emerge from the same prism.

BEYOND GENDER

I have often been asked: Why wasn't there a woman Baal Shem Tov? Why isn't there a woman Rebbe? Why should women rely on male insights with regard to their development as females?

I always answer that these questions don't bother me. Were there to be a woman Baal Shem Tov, I would admire her as a teacher and as a spiritual guide because of her insight and the depth of her character, not because she was a female. For me, the profound insight and spiritual purpose that the Baal Shem Tov and the Rebbe communicate make the above questions seem out of place.

We have been taught to[2] "accept the truth from whoever says it." The insights which the Rebbe has shared with us help us grow in all dimensions, enabling us to become more of ourselves. For a woman, that means cultivating a greater

---

2.   Old adage, cited by *Rambam* in his Introduction to Tractate *Avos.*

awareness of all aspects of her personality, including those which express her femininity.

THE WOMAN'S VOICE WITHIN US

There are thus two ways to conceive of women's liberation: (a) seeking equality within the masculine world; (b) liberating the feminine aspects of our personality and manifesting them. The latter conception reflects the thrust of the Rebbe's directives for women. The Rebbe has always seen every individual as a full person, to be gently but firmly encouraged to fulfill herself or himself.

In times like ours when people are struggling to find a true sense of self, and are feeling a need to go beyond themselves, this message is vital. Without discounting the need for equity within the workplace and within society, it is the microcosm, the individual person, who influences the macrocosm, society at large.[3] And in seeking self-fulfillment ourselves, and in endeavoring to build a society which encourages such efforts, it is important to hear the woman's voice within us, and to let the world at large hear it, too.

In the works of our Sages, and particularly in the Kabbalah, certain qualities of character are described as masculine and others as feminine. These definitions are not

---

3. The question, however, remains: What is the most effective way to secure fair opportunity and equal rights for women? Though there is no easy answer to that question, one thing is clear. The external climate cannot change radically before the internal climate does. As long as people cling to their old sets of values, their reaction to women will be scripted into them regardless of whether or not the constitution is amended to protect women's rights.

   One of the frequently-repeated slogans of Women's Lib was, "The personal is political"; i.e., the functioning of our personal lives is often determined by larger, political forces. The converse is also true, and indeed, perhaps a more dynamic statement of truth. "The political is personal"; society will change when people do.

mutually exclusive. On the contrary, our character traits are interrelated.[4] Nevertheless, though every masculine trait has within it a feminine dimension, and every feminine trait has a masculine side, the basic concept remains, that there exist feminine and masculine ways of thinking and feeling.[5]

Which traits are defined as feminine? Our Sages tell us[6] that women are more richly endowed with *Binah* than men. Generally, *Binah* is translated as "understanding". More particularly, it refers to one's ability to interlock ideas and connect them, thereby developing a concept in all its particulars. But more important than the fact that the faculty of *Binah* allows us to see all the pieces of a puzzle, *Binah* brings these pieces close to our attention and enables us to identify with them.

CONNECTED KNOWLEDGE

This feminine approach to thinking is becoming increasingly important in our lives today. The intelligence revolution exposes us to an ever-surging sea of information. Formidable waves of data come upon us cold and impersonal, and

---

4. *Tanya*, ch. 3.
5. These concepts are reflected in much of the "new feminist" literature being published today. Psychological studies in books with titles like *Women's Ways of Knowing* and *In a Different Voice* point to divergent conceptual approaches between women and men.

    Moreover, there are studies that suggest that these differences are not merely psychological in origin, but reflect actual physiological differences between a woman's brain and a man's. For example: In women, the corpus colossum, the part of the brain which allows for lateralization (the communication between the right and left sides of the brain), is significantly larger than in men.

    Nevertheless, no matter how widely accepted, these findings are subject (as are all hypotheses of secular science) to debate, and serious objections to them have been raised. It is too early to conclude that contemporary science echoes the Torah's conception of the workings of a woman's mind or heart.
6. *Niddah* 45b.

the constant and ever-more-urgent need to process it on a day-to-day basis, dwarfs our sense of self. We all feel the need to balance the technological advances that have become part of our lives, with growth on the human side.

And this is where a woman's added dimension of *Binah* is most significant. It gives a woman a greater tendency toward empathy and what sociologists call "connected knowledge." A woman arrives at knowledge by establishing a personal bond with the idea she wants to discover; she makes it part of herself, instead of treating it as merely an abstract construct.

All around us, we see people looking for this type of change. The success of Outward Bound and other wilderness groups (and the appeal they have for women as well as for men) indicates how strongly people desire to get back into touch with nature. The pet industry is flourishing, as people seek to somehow tap into the life-force of animals. And in our families, in our workplaces, and with friends, the importance of communication skills is being increasingly stressed.

A woman's nature gives her the potential to exercise leadership in this area, and to engender warmth and trust in human relations. And as we strive to be more human, we will also develop a sensitivity to concepts which transcend humanity and thus attune ourselves to the spiritual.

A LASTING CONTRIBUTION

Women have made great advances in the last generation, achieving success within the traditional roles offered by contemporary society. We have gotten a greater share of the pie, only to ask ourselves whether the pie is spiced to our tastes. As women experience a wider range of employment options, they often wonder if they want to continue at jobs which have mounting pressures and time demands. Indeed, many men are opting out and seeking to simplify their lives and devote more time to their families.

The busy routines we follow should not be allowed to rob us of the flexibility to rethink our priorities and, if necessary, redefine them. Our culture extols wealth and power, but in the midst of their pursuit, many of us realize that some of the most important things in life have absolutely nothing to do with these factors.[7]

We all have a desire for achievement, to make our mark on humanity, and to contribute something to posterity. Be it a building to design, a book to write, or an advance in medical technology, all of us, men and women, want to add something to our world. Women, however, have the unique potential to focus on the human being who lives on the 24th story of the building, on the person who will read the book, and on the quality of the life that the medical advance will save.

My mother-in-law understood this well. She used to smile and say, "I brought four children into the world and raised them to be healthy in mind and in body, and well-adjusted. Now, *that's* a lasting contribution to society."

Breathing humanity into the lives of our families is a self-perpetuating cycle. For well-adjusted children grow into well-adjusted parents who will raise well-adjusted children. And this is true outside the home as well. Touching the human side of a person makes him or her more capable of touching the human side of others.

It isn't an either/or choice; ours is a world of multiple options. Whether she pursues a career outside the home, or

---

7. This thinking, too, is apparent in much of the recent feminist literature which seeks to define a second stage of the movement that will enable women to develop themselves as individuals and communicate more effectively with others.

makes her home her career, or fuses the two, a woman's unique gift is to develop the human potential that she possesses, together with the potential which is found within her husband, within her children, and within all the people with whom she comes in contact.

I am not suggesting that women should forfeit the opportunities which contemporary life presents. What I would like to encourage is that we advance as women, use the unique gifts which we have been granted to enhance the humanity of our lives and the lives of the people around us, and make ourselves more sensitive to the inner spiritual truth that is present in every element of existence.

Our Sages[8] describe how during the time of Korach's rebellion against the leadership of Moshe Rabbeinu, Ohn ben Peles found himself involved in this unproductive public controversy. His wife is held up for praise as having saved him. She had the foresight to look beyond the immediacies of his predicament; scorning a life of prestige, she even risked her own reputation in order to secure a life of meaning with her husband and family. Summing up her wise choice, the Sages pay her the ultimate compliment by applying to her the verse,[9] "The wisdom of a woman builds her home."

Woman's wisdom of this kind is particularly important today in building our homes and families. Women have an inner sense of their own future and that of their families. Navigating according to this sense, they endeavor to inculcate lasting meaning and purpose in those around them.

---

8.   *Sanhedrin* 109b; *Bamidbar Rabbah* 18:20.
9.   *Mishlei* 14:1.

HOMEMAKING AND HOUSEKEEPING

Back in the mid-seventies, a Rabbi I know was speaking to a group of students about women's issues. In the middle of the discussion one lively young woman confronted him sharply: "Rabbi, what does your wife do?"

On the one hand, there may not have been room for that question. After all, they were talking in the abstract, about how women and men should live their lives; surely there was no need to touch on the personal affairs of anyone involved. On the other hand, what the woman was really saying was, "Rabbi, if your abstracts are not reflected in your personal life, then I'm not interested!"

The Rabbi answered her that his wife managed a home for eight unwanted children. To these children she was everything — mother, counselor, teacher, social worker.

His listeners glowed. Here, at last, was a Rabbi whose wife had a career. *She* was not shackled to her home. As they continued talking, however, they realized that those eight children were the Rabbi's and his wife's, and the home she managed was their own.

They protested. Firstly, the Rabbi had misled them. Secondly, his wife did fit the stereotype — a typical Rabbi's wife, stuck at home with nothing to do but care for the children.

The Rabbi listened and smiled: "When you thought that my wife ran a home for others, it was okay. But when she runs her own home, it's no longer good enough."

Homemaking is a career, and mothering is a career. And both — or either — of these two careers can contribute to a woman's sense of fulfillment.

Homemaking is not housekeeping. Homemaking means determining the atmosphere of the house, defining its rhythms, its basic thrust and character. Housekeeping means keeping it neat and tidy. Housekeepers, either male or female, can be hired. Homemaking is a challenge which every individual must face personally.

One couple, both academics, began their careers as traveling lecturers. They would journey from campus to campus, staying at each destination for only a short while. Rather than invest in buying a house, they made their home in a trailer.

They had a child, who shared in both the positive dimensions of their living experience, and the challenges it presented. Once at a get-together of their extended family, one of the little girl's uncles asked her: "Honey, aren't you sorry you don't have a home?"

To which she replied: "But Uncle Sam, we do have a home. We just don't have a house to put it in."

Homemaking is a combined effort to which both husband and wife must contribute. Nevertheless, it is the woman who is called[10] *akeres habayis*, a term which can be understood as *ikaro shel bayis* — "the mainstay of the home." For the heightened *Binah* and the connected knowledge that women possess enable them to weave abstract values and spiritual principles into the palpable fabric of the home environment. Without minimizing the role a man must play in cultivating the environment of his home, it is a woman who nurtures and shapes that environment on a day-to-day basis.

As an example of this, the Sages[11] point out that though a man may give a pauper money, his wife's charity is superior: by sharing her handiwork with the pauper, she is the first to satisfy his hunger. In other household dynamics likewise, it is the woman whose skill shapes raw materials into beneficial products.

---

10. *Tehillim* 113:9.
11. *Taanis* 23b.

This contribution is not necessarily dependent on whether a woman stays home, or whether she has a career outside; it has to do with how much of herself she invests in her home. There are women who are at home all day and yet cannot summon up the inner energy to be homemakers, and there are others who give of themselves both at home and in their workplaces.

INVESTING IN CHILDREN

On the verse,[12] "A man will... cleave to his wife and they will become a single flesh," *Rashi* explains that it is in the birth of children that the union of a man and a woman is consummated. And so, having and raising children is a fundamental component of the way a couple shape their home environment.

This is a natural drive within a woman. Caring for your own baby inspires an inner satisfaction that rings true. Children have always been considered one of the greatest blessings a couple can be granted. And the more children, the greater the blessing.[13]

Mothering is a continuation of homemaking. If homemaking means investing yourself in your environment, mothering means making such an investment within our children. And the two go hand in hand; as a woman molds her own home environment, she is shaping that of her children.

It is in mothering that the difference between homemaking and housekeeping becomes crucial. True enough, a child needs a housekeeper, someone to make sure he is fed, clothed, and kept clean. But together with these material

---

12. *Bereishis* 2:24.
13. See the essay below entitled "Family Planning."

things, his parents must invest in his character, and endow him with values, principles and purpose. If their tangible gifts are not coupled with intangible ones, the children may grow up deprived. And this kind of deprivation in a child's formative years is very hard to compensate for in later life.

Gently and patiently, a mother nurtures her child's self-assurance and growth as a person from the tiniest age. For the child's education begins far before she or he enters a schoolroom. Her or his character and personality are being molded from the moment she or he emerges into the world and begins interacting with the environment. Indeed, even within the fetal environment of the womb, education is taking place.

Here the reassuring love of a mother is all-important. A mother's loving bond with her baby convinces that child that the world can be a rewarding place to live in. The absence of such love can leave a child with the sense that the world at large is unsatisfying, challenging, and even hostile.

Without a mothering influence, even when their rearing is entrusted to professionals, children grow up lacking. This has been documented in studies of children raised on kibbutzim and communes. Indeed, on the basis of these studies, the kibbutz movement has rethought its ideology towards home and family.

G-D NEEDS HOMEMAKERS

The art and skill of homemaking is metaphorically relevant beyond the individual sphere of our own homes. Indeed, our Sages explain[14] that G-d created the world because He desired a home.

---

14. *Midrash Tanchuma, Parshas Bechukosai,* sec. 3.

What does this analogy mean? A home is where we relax and express ourselves. This is possible outside our homes as well, but it is not the same. There are always social conventions, personal reservations, and the like. But when we're at home, it's different. That's where we can really express who we are.

G-d created our world to be His home, the place where He expresses who He really is. Nevertheless, the headlines of any newspaper make it clear that, as of yet, this is merely a potential. It is a sizable challenge to make the world we live in fit to be a dwelling for mortals, let alone for G-d. It will not be until the Era of the Redemption that we will actually be able to see just how the world is His home.

G-d has left the task of cultivating the environment of His home to mankind, to become His homemakers by refining our conduct. And just as the major role in modulating the environment of our own homes has been entrusted to women, so too, womanly traits — the insights of connected knowledge inspired by a woman's heightened measure of *Binah* — are vital in the task of transforming the world into a home where G-d can express Himself.

THE MARRIAGE OF G-D AND HIS PEOPLE

The male and female aspects of the relationship between G-d and the Jewish people, and their respective roles in the dynamic of perfecting the world, are reflected in the *Song of Songs*. Our Sages explain[15] that the lyrical resonance of its classical Hebrew communicates more than a message of sensuous love: it is a saga of the ongoing relationship between G-d and His people. The love depicted there, now waxing, now waning, serves as an allegory for the alternating states of

---

15. Cf. *Yadayim* 3:5; *Rashi* on *Shir HaShirim* 1:1.

exile and redemption that our people have experienced over the years.

Though at the superficial level of analogy this is a description of human love, in this case the analogy and the analogue are one and the same. For in composing the *Song of Songs*, King Solomon intended to motivate the full range of our personalities, not only our minds. He wanted us to know how deep and powerful is the relationship that the Jewish people share with G-d.

The *Zohar*[16] teaches that G-d created our world "in order that we know Him": everything He brought into being is a bugle to awaken within us a deeper understanding of our relationship with Him.

The objects and people in our physical world thus mean more than what meets the eye; they are merely palpable echoes of spiritual realities. It is not only that they enable us to gain an awareness of the spiritual; the truth of their existence is the spiritual truth that they echo. Their physical existence is merely a garment that enables these spiritual truths to be expressed in material terms.[17]

If this is true about creation as a whole, it is surely true of the fundamental element of creation — man. Thus, for example, the relationship between a man and a woman mirrors the bond between G-d and man.

In essence, a husband and a wife are one being; indeed, the *Zohar*[18] describes their union as the joining of two half-souls. Nevertheless, this deep-seated oneness does not always surface. As husbands and wives live their lives from day to day, they often see themselves primarily as separate entities

---

16. II, 42b.
17. See the *maamar* entitled *Veyadaata 5657* (English translation entitled *To Know G-d*; Kehot, N.Y., 1993).
18. III, 7b, 109b; see *Yevamos* 63a.

who still need to cultivate and nurture the love that should join them.

Similar concepts apply with regard to G-d and His people. Every element of existence contains a spark of G-dliness. In particular, our Jewish soul is[19] "truly a part of G-d above." Nevertheless, we are usually conscious of our own individual personalities, and not of that G-dly core. Developing a bond with G-d requires effort.

The *Song of Songs* tells us about a process of developing harmony — on one level, between a man and a woman, and on a deeper level, between G-d and His people. It explains how sometimes it is the man (in the analogue, G-d) who takes the initiative, and sometimes, it is the woman (the Jewish people), and how sometimes their periods of closeness are disrupted by an inability to communicate. It concludes with an allegorical promise that ultimately, in the Era of Redemption, the loving bond between G-d and His people will blossom into fulfillment.

SEEING THE FUTURE IN THE PRESENT

In the Torah,[20] love is called "knowledge". This implies looking at one's partner up close, seeing him (or her) as he really is, and opening oneself to him. Significantly, however, when the analogy in the *Song of Songs* speaks of a deep and lasting love, it often describes not a state of closeness, but a love that thrives despite distance and separation. The same applies in the analogue. The woman in the analogy says,[21] "I am asleep, yet my heart is awake." In this verse the Sages[22] hear the self-assuring words of Israel during the time of exile:

---

19. See *Tanya*, ch. 2, paraphrasing *Iyov* 31:2.
20. Cf. *Bereishis* 4:1, *et al.*
21. *Shir HaShirim* 5:2.
22. *Yalkut Shimoni* on *Shir HaShirim*, *Remez* 988.

"I am asleep from the Redemption, yet my heart is awake to G-d."

This ability to feel a powerful love despite separation, comes naturally to women. Women are plainly in touch with the reality in which they live. Nevertheless, the scope of their conception is not narrowed by this awareness; they are able to see beyond the immediacies of their environment.

This potential is exemplified in the narrative of our people's exile and redemption in ancient Egypt. Our Sages relate[23] that, wearied by the pressures of forced labor, and in despair because of Pharaoh's decree to drown their sons in the Nile, our forefathers would have refrained from bringing more children into the world. Their wives, however, refused to resign themselves to such a situation, and gently awakened their husbands' love.

They knew how hard their husbands worked — indeed, they too were forced to perform hard labor; they also knew of Pharaoh's cruel decree. But they understood that the exile was only temporary, whereas the love between a husband and a wife, and the conception of children, are permanent values. And they knew that ultimately, what was of permanent value would prevail.

Our Sages teach us,[24] "In the merit of righteous women, our ancestors were redeemed from Egypt." What was the women's merit? — That they were able to look beyond the darkness and suffering around them. For them, redemption was not a promise of the future; it was a real factor in their lives. This gave them the inner strength to raise children who were able to "recognize G-d first" at the Red Sea.[25] In

---

23. *Sotah* 11b, commenting on *Shir HaShirim* 8:5.
24. *Sotah, loc. cit.*
25. *Ibid.*; *Shmos Rabbah* 23:8. Even the youngest infants joined in the song of redemption (*Sotah* 30b).

the same way, every Jew possesses faith — not as a learnt trait, but as an inherent expression of his true identity. Since his soul is a spark of G-d, every individual's awareness of spirituality rings true within his or her inner being.[26]

A woman's nature makes this goal particularly attainable. This does not mean that she will not face challenges and require effort to overcome them. Rather, her unique tendency to be in touch with her inner self, enables her to focus on values that are true and lasting and ultimately to bring them into expression.

A RESPONSIVE HEART

Our Sages have told us that the time before the coming of *Mashiach* will be a time of paradox. On the one hand, we will be able to perceive a glimmer of the future light. On the other hand, this era will be weighted down by a darkness so palpable that it will prevent the light from being properly perceived.[27]

Our Prophets[28] allude to this state by referring to the struggles which will precede the Redemption as *chevlei Mashiach*, the birthpangs of *Mashiach*. All women who have given birth will agree that the exhilaration of bringing new life into the world dwarfs the intensity of the pain, however great. The birth itself is the most powerful dimension of the entire experience, and the most lasting.

---

26. *Tanya*, ch. 42.
27. See, for example, *Zohar Chadash* (*Bereishis* 6:1) on the "darkness beyond darkness" that will befall our people before the sun of redemption shines forth. So, too, commenting on the end of *Parshas Shmos*, the *Kli Yakar* writes that "every day, close to dawn, the darkness is at its deepest.... Similarly, in the winter, close to sunrise, the cold becomes stronger and is eventually conquered by the sun."
28. Cf. *Hoshea* 13:13; *Yeshayahu* 37:3, 66:8.

The changes taking place throughout our society on both the global and the individual planes point to a transition of awesome scope. As in the experience of giving birth, women focus on the ultimate goal of this transition, the coming of the Redemption, and are not overwhelmed by the magnitude of the challenges this transition presents. Moreover, a woman's sense of forevision enables her to bring the awareness of the Redemption into her life today. For the essence of the Era of the Redemption is the fusion of the material and the spiritual — that we do not see the world as an independent physical entity, but appreciate its inner spiritual content. And such an approach is natural for a woman.

In this spirit the Prophet Yeshayahu tells us that when *Mashiach* comes,[29] "The world will be filled with the knowledge of G-d as the waters cover the ocean bed." We will know G-d, not as an abstract, spiritual entity, but as an integral part of every dimension of our lives.

When speaking of the Jewish people at the time of the Redemption, the Prophet Yechezkel says:[30] "I will remove the heart of stone from their flesh, and give them a heart of flesh." What the prophet is saying is that a sensitive heart, a heart that responds to what the mind knows, is the key to the change in our feelings that will take place in the Era of the Redemption.

We do not have to wait for the Redemption to begin developing such sensitivity. We can begin removing the hardness from our hearts already.[31] Indeed, *living with the*

---

29. *Yeshayahu* 11:9.
30. *Yechezkel* 11:19.
31. At the age of forty, as the Sages testify, Rabbi Akiva was still an unlearned man. One day, while tending his flock, he noticed that the stones of a well had been worn away by dripping water. This led him to the understanding that the Torah (which is likened to water; cf. the commentaries to *Yeshayahu* 55:1; *Bava Kama* 17a, *et al.*) could modify and refine those aspects of his nature that were as rough as stone (*Avos deRabbi Nasan* 6:2).

Redemption — anticipating its effects by sensitizing our lives right now — serves as a catalyst that will make the Redemption a foreseeable and manifest reality.[32] Thinking over the Rebbe's insights and applying them in our lives are fundamental elements in this process. Each of the essays to follow heightens our awareness of the potentials we possess as women, and points towards realistic goals for the expression of these potentials. In this way, they spur us to summon up and channel positive energies to enhance our lives and those of our families and friends, making Redemption a reality.

On the place of women in Torah study, see the essay below entitled, "The Right to Know."

32. Since the Divine response to mortal initiatives follows the principle of "measure for measure" (*Nedarim* 24a), the coming of the time when we will perceive the G-dly core of all existence will be precipitated by the steps that people make in that direction at present.

Part I:
Womanhood

Social Involvement Enhanced by Modesty

LIBERATING ONE'S FEMININITY

Today,[1] man is being granted ever-increasing potentials. Advances in technology and communications enable us to shape our environment and share ideas with people throughout the world far more effectively than ever before. Similarly, in the realm of personal relations, many social barriers have been dropped. Interpersonal differences that used to obstruct the flow of commerce and information are falling away and there is a greater willingness to accept a person without discrimination.

This also applies to differences in sex. Being now less restricted than in previous generations, women are accepting greater participatory roles in every area of social life. In the face of these changes, a Jewish woman might ask herself: "Are these changes positive? Should the opportunities available be accepted, or should they be rejected as part of the

---

1.   A recurring theme — the delicate tension between the increasingly partici-
     patory roles now open to women, and the due demands of feminine modesty
     — figured in talks of the Rebbe on the fourth and seventh nights of Sukkos
     and again on *Shabbos Parshas Noach*, 5751 [1990]. Excerpts from these talks
     are adapted in the above essay.

challenges of contemporary society that conflict with our traditional values?"

The Torah's response to these questions involves a delicate balance between these stances. In principle, a woman need not shy away from involvement in the world. Nevertheless, that involvement need not indiscriminately mimic the norms of society at large, but rather should be flavored by the unique approach of *tzniyus* which the Torah teaches.

Tzniyus (lit., "modesty") does not imply merely a code of rules for dress and conduct. Rather, it stands for an outlook, an approach to life that expresses a woman's femininity and distinctive inner nature. In the words of the Psalms,[2] "All the glory of the king's daughter is inward *(pnimah)*." In other words, women are endowed with a unique potential — to contribute a dimension of inwardness *(pnimiyus)* to their homes, to the people with whom they come in contact, and to their respective environments.

CREATING A DWELLING FOR G-D

Further insights into this dimension can be derived from the narrative of creation, in which the Creator of both man and woman gave them directives to guide their conduct. The Torah relates that after creating man and woman, G-d blessed them and charged them,[3] "Be fruitful and multiply, fill the land and conquer it."

Our Sages note that in the word וכבשה ("and conquer it"), the Torah omits the expected letter *vav* (before the final *hei*), which would normally indicate that a plural audience is being addressed; instead, the directive is spelled as if addressed to a singular, male listener. It can thus be under-

---

2.   *Tehillim* 45:14.
3.   *Bereishis* 1:28.

stood to be addressed to the man alone, for[4] "a man has a tendency to conquer, whereas a woman does not have a tendency to conquer."

Our Sages understand the "conquest" of this world as referring to man's endeavors to harness it and transform it into a dwelling place for G-d. That is to say: We can transform the world into a place where G-d's essence is openly manifest, in the same way that any individual manifests his essential personality totally and freely in his own home.

When explained in this context, our Sages' restriction of the task of "conquering" the world to men is problematic. On the contrary, surely the greatest manifestation of this form of divine service is reflected in a woman's efforts to make her home into[5] "a sanctuary in microcosm," transforming the material elements of her household into a dwelling place for Him. There is no place where this sanctification of our mundane realities is expressed so richly as in a Jewish home.

One resolution of this difficulty revolves around the conception of man and woman as a single unit. In the words of the Torah,[6] "G-d said, 'Let us make man...'; ...man and woman He created them." Ever since that moment, only when man and woman unite are they a complete entity; alone, each is only[7] "half a person." Thus, there is no need for a separate command for a woman. Her activity is part of her ongoing partnership with her husband. Moreover, their efforts in "conquering" the world depend on her, for until a desirable environment in his own home is established, a person's service in the world at large will be deficient. To

---

4. *Yevamos* 65b.
5. *Yechezkel* 11:16.
6. *Bereishis* 1:26-27.
7. *Zohar* III, 7b; 109b; 296a. Indeed the *Midrash* conceives of a primordial stage in the creation of man — a composite of two faces, back to back, later separated into man and woman. (See *Bereishis Rabbah* 8:1, cited in *Rashi* on *Bereishis* 1:27.)

express this idea in allegory, only a foolish king would go out to conquer other countries before mastering his own.[8]

COMMUNICATION VS. CONQUEST

The restriction to men of the command to "conquer" the world may also be understood at a deeper level. A woman's sphere of influence, like a man's, also extends beyond the home. Nevertheless, she exerts this influence in a distinctive manner, different to that exerted by men. A man often tries to conquer, i.e., to confront and overpower other individuals. In contrast, a woman typically presents a concept tranquilly and peaceably, with modest understatement, thus more effectively allowing her listeners to join her in appreciating its worth.

To explain this concept using chassidic terminology: The difference between *malchus* ("sovereignty") and *memshalah* ("dominion") lies in the manner in which they are secured. *Malchus* refers to a situation in which a nation willingly accepts the authority of a king; to borrow a phrase from the liturgy,[9] "His children beheld His might... and willingly accepted His sovereignty." In contrast, *memshalah* refers to power which is acquired by force, against the will of the populace.

Malchus possesses a twofold advantage. Firstly, when a people willingly accept their king's authority, they are less likely to rebel. There is, however, a deeper aspect: in this manner, a people's connection to their king is not merely

---

8. Cf. *Sifri* on *Parshas Eikev*, sec. 51, as cited in *Tosafos* on *Avodah Zarah* 21a, s.v. *Kibush yachid*.
9. *Siddur Tehillat HaShem*, p. 109.

external, but part and parcel of their own being. It is their minds and wills which accept him.[10]

Men often choose to influence their environment by force. Thus, although they may attain their goals, the manner in which they secure their conquest may cause friction with those around them. In contrast, the inner dimension (pnimiyus) which characterizes a woman's approach[11] makes the ideas which she presents attractive to others and causes them to be accepted as part of their own perspective. Indeed, many men would be well advised to learn this approach from women and incorporate it in their own life-work.

INNER BEAUTY: TZNIYUS TODAY

The inwardness of a woman's approach depends on tzniyus. The manner in which a woman presents herself teaches people to appreciate inward rather than outward beauty; it allows people to appreciate the inner dimensions of her personality.

In recent years, the trend in society at large appears to be turning toward this approach. This positive direction should be enhanced even further, for the nature of the advances women have made in society has created both new difficulties and new solutions to them.[12]

---

10. See *Likkutei Torah*, *Devarim*, p. 1b, which explains these concepts within the context of the acceptance of the yoke of G-d's Kingship.
11. There is an intrinsic connection between women and sovereignty; indeed, in the terminology of the *Kabbalah*, woman serves as a metaphor for the *Sefirah* of *Malchus*.
12. For example, since a woman's sphere of influence has been extended beyond her home and family, she often needs to travel in a taxi alone. Were she to travel with a male driver, questions might arise concerning the prohibition of *yichud* (being alone with a person of the opposite sex). At any rate, a certain measure of modesty is no doubt compromised in such a trip. Nevertheless, the very phenomenon which creates the difficulty — the wider and

As our Sages teach,[13] "By virtue of the righteous women of that generation, the Children of Israel were redeemed from Egypt." Similarly, the qualities of *tzniyus* and inwardness which increasingly characterize the lifestyle of Jewish women in our generation will help transform the world into a dwelling place for G-d, and thus hasten the revelation of His presence, through the coming of *Mashiach*.[14] May this take place in the immediate future.[15]

more varied roles women are taking in our society — often offers a solution. In this instance, it is possible to travel with a woman taxi driver. Even if it takes a little longer to find or order such a driver, it is preferable to make such a sacrifice, in order to develop the dimension of *tzniyus* and inwardness spoken of above.

13. *Sotah* 11b.

14. This is reflected in the statement of the *AriZal* (in *Shaar HaGilgulim*, Second Prelude) that the final generation before the coming of *Mashiach* will be a reincarnation of the generation which left Egypt.

15. At the *farbrengen* of *Yud-Beis* Tammuz, 5724 [1964], the Rebbe cited the *Tosafos* (*Sotah* 14a, *s.v. Mipnei mah*) which speaks of the never-ending need to undo the damage done to our people by the episode of the daughters of Moav (*Bamidbar* 25:1-3). This episode, the ultimate in immodesty, arose out of a challenge to everything that Moshe Rabbeinu stood (and stands) for; its result was mass idolatry.

At the above-mentioned *farbrengen*, the Rebbe explained how the ability to rectify this multiple damage is the unique prerogative of Jewish women — through values which are the reverse of the above, and especially through *tzniyus*, the kind of inwardness that enables a woman to infuse her home with appropriate content. For the founding of such miniature sanctuaries by Jewish women everywhere prepares the entire world for the construction of the ultimate Sanctuary, the Third *Beis HaMikdash* in Jerusalem, with the coming of *Mashiach*.

A Woman Called Esther

WHAT'S IN A NAME?

Esther's preeminent role is highlighted in the very name of the *Megillah*, the Biblical Scroll which recounts the Purim narrative.[1] It is not called *"Megillas Mordechai"* or *"Megillas Mordechai and Esther"* or even *"Megillas Esther and Mordechai."* It is called simply *"Megillas Esther."*

Though it was indisputably Esther who actually moved Achashverosh to act, Mordechai also played a role in the salvation. Indeed, the *Megillah* testifies that he was the dominant force behind Esther. In fact, she is first introduced in the *Megillah* in terms of her relationship to Mordechai:[2] "He had brought up Hadassah, that is, Esther, his uncle's daughter." Her every action was based on Mordechai's

---

1. The prime mortal architect of the miracle of Purim was Esther. In the course of this episode, which took place in early Second Temple times, the Jews dispersed throughout the 127 provinces of the Persian Empire were saved from the anti-Semitic designs of Haman, grand vizier to King Achashverosh (Ahasuerus). Risking her life for her people, Queen Esther braved the King's anger and entreated him to have pity on them. As the *Megillah* records, she was eminently successful.

    The above text summarizes a talk of the Rebbe on *Shabbos Parshas Tzav*, 13 of Adar II, 5744 [1984], in connection with the Week of the Jewish Woman.

2. *Esther* 2:7.

advice:[3] "Esther would carry out the bidding of Mordechai."
Her supreme moment, when she was to go to the King to
plead for her people, took place only at Mordechai's instiga-
tion and virtual command. So reluctant was she to go that
Mordechai had to speak harshly:[4] "If you remain silent at this
time, relief and deliverance shall arise for the Jews from
another place, while you and your father's house shall perish.
And who knows whether you did not come to royal estate for
just such a time as this?"

Since Mordechai thus played a critical role not only in
Esther's life but also in the national crisis, should not the
Megillah, which narrates the events of the danger and the
subsequent salvation, be named after both of the chief participants in the salvation, Esther and Mordechai?

MORDECHAI AND ESTHER: TORAH AND JEWRY

This question can be resolved by seeing Mordechai and
Esther not only as individuals, but also as personifications of
the Torah and the Jewish people, respectively. Our Sages
affirm:[5] "Mordechai in his generation was equal to Moshe in
his generation.... Just as Moshe taught the Torah to Israel,...
so did Mordechai." Esther, the *Talmud* teaches,[6] was called
Hadassah "after the righteous who are called myrtles *(hadas)*"
— and[7] "Your people are *all* righteous." On one level, the
Torah, personified in the *Megillah* by Mordechai, transcends
Israel, personified by Esther, for Israel must follow the
Torah's directives. In the words of the *Megillah*,[8] "Esther
(Israel) would carry out the bidding of Mordechai (the

---

3.   *Ibid.* 2:20.
4.   *Ibid.* 4:14.
5.   *Esther Rabbah* 6:2.
6.   *Megillah* 13a.
7.   *Yeshayahu* 60:21.
8.   *Esther* 2:20.

Torah)." Indeed, the Torah is the medium which brings to light the unique distinction of Jews.

On the other hand, once the distinctive qualities of the Jewish people have been revealed by means of their identification with the Torah, their innate superiority blazes forth, and Israel is seen to be loftier even than the Torah. As our Sages have said,[9] the Divine intent of creating Israel came to mind, so to speak, before anything else, even before the Torah.

In words of a different flavor: The Baal Shem Tov compares the Jewish people to a land filled with precious resources, as in the verse,[10] "You shall be a land of delight." Every Jew possesses valuable qualities and virtues; but these treasures are buried deep within him, and persistent toil is needed to bring them to light — just as one must dig deep to uncover the precious metals and gems in the earth. Once the concealing strata have been removed, a Jew's innate qualities shine forth.

The same may be said of Mordechai and Esther as individuals, in their roles in the story of Purim. Mordechai, it is true, had to persuade Esther to do her part in removing the decree against the Jews. But Mordechai did not need to effect any basic change in her. His function was only to reveal her innate qualities, to allow her real self to surface. And once he succeeded in doing this, Esther set out on her mission with her own strength, impelled by her own convictions. At this point, she became the direct cause of the miracle.

For in her true and innate state which was now revealed, Esther stood on a higher rung than Mordechai. It was she who now took the initiative to tell Mordechai,[11] "Go, gather

---

9.   *Bereishis Rabbah* 1:4.
10. *Malachi* 3:12.
11. *Esther* 4:16.

all the Jews to be found in Shushan, and fast for me." And it was Esther who convinced the Sages of her time to include the *Megillah* as one of the sacred writings of the *Tanach*.[12]

The miracle of Purim thus came about through Esther's own innate qualities, albeit after Mordechai revealed them. Moreover, those qualities were infinitely superior to Mordechai's, just as Jewry in essence is infinitely loftier than the Torah. For these reasons, *Megillas Esther* is named solely after her.

A LESSON FROM THE MEGILLAH

The Baal Shem Tov offered a unique interpretation of the *mishnah* which states,[13] "One who reads the *Megillah* backwards has not discharged his obligation." That is to say: If one reads the *Megillah* thinking that the events related in it happened only in the past ("backwards") and are not relevant today, he has missed the entire point of the reading — to learn how a Jew should conduct himself at all times, now as in the past. Hence the importance of noting the name of the *Megillah*, which, as explained above, emphasizes the greatness of a Jewish woman.

Just as our frequent reiteration of the distinctive qualities of Jews is not chauvinism, but is intended to highlight the obligations of Jewry, so the purpose of talking of the greatness of Jewish women is to stress their weighty responsibilities.

Every Jewish woman is the mainstay of her home, who sets the tone and spirit of the entire household. In particular, it is the woman who bears the responsibility of rearing her

---

12. *Megillah* 7a.
13. *Ibid.* 2:1.

children in the traditions of Torah and Judaism, ensuring that they live every aspect of life as Torah Jews.

It is the woman, the constant presence in the home, who has the task of ensuring that the home be pure and sanctified, suffused with the light of Torah and *mitzvos*. In particular, her task is to buttress the three pillars of the Jewish home: the *kashrus* of the food consumed, the kindling of the *Shabbos* and *Yom-Tov* lights, and the bringing of children into the world in the spirit of the laws of family purity,[14] together with their subsequent upbringing.

ORAH: TORAH

The characteristic qualities of the Jewish woman recall the verse in the *Megillah*,[15] "For the Jews there was *orah* ('light')," which alludes to the Torah.[16] Now *or*, which also means "light", refers to the Written Torah. Why does the *Megillah* choose to refer to the Torah as *orah* (using the feminine form of that word), which refers to the Oral Torah?

G-d's Will is expressed in both the Written and the Oral Torah. However, as the Alter Rebbe writes,[17] "the Supreme Will as vested in the 613 commandments of the Written Torah, is hidden and covered, secreted and concealed. It is manifest only in the Oral Torah." The Written Torah, for example, says of the *mitzvah* of *tefillin* that[18] "You shall bind them as a sign on your arm, and they shall be for frontlets between your eyes." What exactly this instruction means, and just how it is to be fulfilled, remains obscure until it is clarified in the Oral Torah. In the metaphorical language of

---

14. See the essay below entitled "Family Planning."
15. *Esther* 8:16.
16. *Megillah* 16b.
17. *Tanya* — *Iggeres HaKodesh*, Epistle 29. (See *Lessons In Tanya*, Vol. V, p. 221.)
18. *Devarim* 6:8.

the *Kabbalah*, the Oral Law fulfills the characteristically feminine function of unfolding each seminal teaching and nurturing it into full flower in all its tangible detail.

It was therefore the Oral Torah, whose laws enable Jews to fulfill the Divine Will on a practical level, that was Haman's chief target.[19] Hence, when his decree was frustrated, "for the Jews there was *orah*" — the light radiated by the Oral Torah, against which his decree was primarily directed. Purim thus highlights action, the translation of the Supreme Will into actual practice, and it is the Oral Torah which enables a Jew to do this through the observance of the commandments.

This, then, is the connection of the Oral Torah to the name of the *Megillah* — not *Megillas Mordechai* or *Megillas Mordechai and Esther*, but simply *Megillas Esther*; and in the *Megillah* the Torah is called only *orah*, using the feminine form of the noun, and not *or*, or both *or* and *orah*.

"These days," the *Megillah* assures us,[20] "are recalled and observed in every generation." In our days, too, the events of Purim again come to life, particularly since Purim teaches an evergreen lesson. As the above verse goes on to say, "These days of Purim shall never cease among the Jews, and their remembrance shall never perish from their descendants."

THE WEEK OF THE JEWISH WOMAN

In the spirit of the above, may it be G-d's will that the Week of the Jewish Woman, whose purpose is to inspire and encourage Jewish women in their faith, and which is being observed at this Purim season, will[21] "benefit themselves and

---

19. Note the charge with which Haman slandered the Jews to Achashverosh ("their laws are different from [those of] every nation"; *Esther* 3:8).
20. *Esther* 9:28.
21. Cf. *Sanhedrin* 71b.

benefit the world." May the deeds of Jewish women illumine the whole world with the light of Torah and *mitzvos*, so that even in these last days of exile G-dliness will be revealed in the world — just as in the era of the Redemption, when[22] "The glory of G-d shall be revealed, and all flesh together shall see that the mouth of G-d has spoken."

---

22. *Yeshayahu* 40:5.

A Partner in
the Dynamic of Creation

THE FEMININE DIMENSION

Our[1] Sages teach that *Shir HaShirim*, the Song of Songs, should not be taken at face value.[2] Rather, it should be understood as an allegory describing the ongoing relationship between G-d and His bride, the Jewish people. The different phases of closeness and separation described in that sacred text serve as analogies for the states of exile our people have suffered and the redemptions that they have experienced — and will yet experience.

The very concept of redemption is intrinsically related to women. Expressed in terms of the Divine emanations known as *Sefiros*, the *Kabbalah* explains[3] that the *Sefirah* of *Malchus*

---

1. The above essay is adapted from talks of the Rebbe on *Shabbos Parshas Bo* (see also the essay below entitled, "A Lifetime Renewed") and on *Parshas Beshalach*, as well as on *Parshas Yisro*, 5752 [1992].

2. The sources for this statement are cited in *Rashi* on *Shir HaShirim* 1:1. See also *Rashi's* characterization of *Shir HaShirim* (in *Berachos* 57a): "Its entire content is the awe of heaven, and the love for G-d in the heart of all of Israel."

3. See *Likkutei Torah, Shir HaShirim*, p. 48b. When considering these Kabbalistic concepts, one should note the *direction* of the chain of causation. It is

(lit., "sovereignty") reflects the feminine dimension. During the periods of exile, *Malchus* is in a state of descent and does not receive a direct downflow of spiritual energy from the higher *Sefiros* with which it is normally linked. Metaphorically, this condition is described as a woman in an enforced state of separation from her husband. Conversely, in the Era of the Redemption,[4] "A woman of valor [will be] the crown of her husband"; the higher source of *Malchus* will be revealed. The direct bond between *Malchus* and the other *Sefiros* will be reestablished,[5] and *Malchus* will become a source of vital influence, renewing the totality of existence.

These concepts have been reflected throughout Jewish history. Our Sages teach that[6] "In the merit of righteous women, the Jews were redeemed from Egypt." The same applies to later redemptions.[7] And as to the future, we have been promised,[8] "As in the days of your Exodus from Egypt, I will show [the people] wonders." The *AriZal*[9] writes that the generation of the ultimate Redemption will be a reincarnation of the generation of the Exodus from Egypt. Since the future Redemption will therefore follow the pattern of that archetypal redemption, it will also come as a result of the merit of the righteous women of that generation.[10]

---

not that the functioning of these spiritual forces *depends* on the situation in the world. On the contrary: their functioning determines it.

4. *Mishlei* 12:4. *Yirmeyahu* 31:21 (see commentaries there) likewise extols the preeminent position of women in the Era of the Redemption.
5. In this context, the Era of the Redemption is referred to as the consummation of the marriage bond between G-d and the Jewish people (*Taanis* 26b).
6. *Sotah* 11b.
7. See *Yalkut Shimoni*, Part II, end of sec. 606.
8. *Michah* 7:15.
9. See *Shaar HaGilgulim, Hakdamah* 20.
10. In this context, we can appreciate the significance of the efforts of the Rebbe Rayatz to encourage the education of Jewish women. See the essay below entitled, "The Right to Know."

A HOME FOR A FAMILY: A SANCTUARY FOR G-D

The role of the Jewish people, G-d's bride, and in particular of Jewish women, in preparing the world for the
Redemption, is analogous to the role of a woman in her own
home. Our Sages[11] teach that G-d created the world so that
He would have a dwelling place among mortals. This ideal
will be fully realized in the Era of the Redemption.[12]

To develop this analogy: A person desires not merely to
possess a dwelling, but that it be attractive and tastefully
furnished. Typically, this task of shaping the home environment is the province of the woman of the house. Similarly,
in the mission of making this world a dwelling for G-d, it is
the Jewish woman who makes His dwelling attractive and
radiant.

This greater role played by women within the world
should also be mirrored in the activity of every woman
within her own home. It is largely through the efforts of the
woman of the house that every home is transformed into[13] "a
sanctuary in microcosm," a place where G-dliness is revealed
in a way which parallels and leads to the revelation that will
permeate the entire world in the Era of the Redemption.

These efforts are reflected, not only in the spiritual influence which a woman instills within the home, but also in
the manner in which she designs its interior — for example,
making sure that every member of the household possesses a
Siddur, a *Chumash*, a *Tanya*, and a *tzedakah pushke* (charity
box) which is proudly displayed.[14] Even the rooms of infants
should be decorated with Jewish symbols, such as a *Shir Ha-*

---

11. *Midrash Tanchuma, Parshas Bechukosai*, sec. 3; *Tanya*, ch. 33.
12. See *Tanya*, ch. 36.
13. *Yechezkel* 11:16.
14. See *Sound the Great Shofar* (Kehot, N.Y., 1992), p. 155.

Maalos.[15] Taken together, these practical endeavors mirror the way in which Judaism permeates even the material environment in which we live.

LIGHTING UP THE HOME:
ILLUMINATING THE SANCTUARY

Shabbos is referred to as[16] "a microcosm of the World to Come," and conversely, the Era of the Redemption is referred to as[17] "the Day which is entirely Shabbos, and repose for life everlasting." On the worldly level, it is the woman of the house who introduces the atmosphere of Shabbos by lighting its Shabbos candles.[18] In this spirit, to recall the analogy of the world as G-d's dwelling, it is the task of women to usher the light of Redemption into the world.

In fact this very mitzvah, the kindling of Shabbos candles, is a powerful medium to accomplish this goal. For the visible light which the candles generate reflects how every mitzvah — and, in a wider sense, every positive activity a Jew initi-

15. This usually takes the form of a decorative poster including Tehillim 121 and sometimes additional texts. (See footnote 16 to the essay below entitled "Three Mothers.")

16. In the original, mei'ein Olam HaBa, a phrase which appears in the zemiros sung at the Shabbos table. Cf.: "The Shabbos is a sixtieth part of the World to Come" (Berachos 57a). This too, like the phrase quoted in our text, alludes to "the World to Come, which is entirely Shabbos" (in the original, HaOlam HaBa, shekulo Shabbos; in Osiyos deRabbi Akiva, sec. 4).

17. In the original, Yom shekulo Shabbos. See the closing words of Tamid 7:4, incorporated in the Sabbath prayer inserted near the conclusion of the Grace after Meals (Siddur Tehillat HaShem, p. 93), which asks that we be privileged to inherit that eternal Day.

18. This recalls the mystical concepts mentioned above. Shabbos also relates to the feminine dimension of the Sefirah of Malchus, as reflected in the expression, "the Shabbos Queen" (in Aramaic, Shabbos Malkesa; see Siddur Tehillat HaShem, p. 132).

ates, such as a friendly word or a kindly deed — increases the G-dly light within the world.[19]

WOMEN AS CATALYSTS OF LIBERATION

The efforts of Jewish women to serve as catalysts for the Redemption have historical precedents. In the Egyptian exile, it was Miriam who relayed the prophecy that a redeemer would emerge.[20] Even when the leaders of that generation could not foresee an end to servitude and oppression, she spread hope and trust among her people.[21]

When her mother was forced to place Moshe, the future redeemer of the Jews, in the Nile, her father Amram approached Miriam and asked her, "What will be the result of your prophecy? How will it be fulfilled?"

Miriam remained at the banks of the Nile and[22] "stood at a distance to know what would happen to him." Our Sages explain that, in addition to her apprehension for her brother's future, she was concerned about the fate of her prophecy. How indeed would the redemption come about?

In a metaphorical sense, this narrative is relevant to all Jewish women, those living at present and those whose souls are in the spiritual realms. Concerned over the fate of the Jewish people, they anxiously await the Redemption: *Ad*

---

19. Cf. *Mishlei* 6:23: "For a *mitzvah* is a lamp, and Torah is light." The analogy of a candle for *mitzvos* is strengthened by the fact that the Hebrew word for "candle" — *ner* (נר), is numerically equivalent to 250. There are 248 positive commandments; when one adds the two basic spiritual emotions of love and awe of G-d, which contribute warmth and vitality to the performance of the *mitzvos*, the sum of 250 is reached.
20. Moreover, this took place while she was still a child, implying that similar activities can be undertaken by Jewish girls even before they reach full maturity.
21. See *Megillah* 11a.
22. *Shmos* 2:4.

Masai! How much longer must the Jewish people remain in exile?[23]

CELEBRATING IN ADVANCE

The anxious anticipation for the redemption felt by Miriam — and by all of the Jewish women in Egypt — was paralleled in its intensity by their exuberant celebration when, after the miracles of the Red Sea, that redemption was consummated. After the men joined Moshe Rabbeinu in song, the women broke out in song and dance,[24] giving thanks to G-d with a spirited rejoicing which surpassed that of the men.

In the very near future, our people will celebrate the coming of the ultimate Redemption, and[25] "The Holy One, blessed be He, will make a dance for the righteous." We can now experience a foretaste of this impending celebration. Although we are still in exile, the confidence that the Redemption is an imminent reality should inspire us with happiness. For the Jewish people have completed all the divine service necessary to bring about the Redemption. To borrow an analogy used by our Sages,[26] the table has already been set

---

23. This plea of all the generations echoes the prayer of Mother Rachel: "A voice is heard in Ramah, lamentation and bitter weeping: Rachel weeping for her children." The reassuring Divine response appears in the continuation of the prophecy: "Your endeavors will be rewarded... and there is hope for your future." And G-d promises further, "Your children shall return to their borders." (See *Rashi* on *Bereishis* 48:7 in reference to *Yirmeyahu* 31:14ff.)

24. The Torah's description of this celebration (*Shmos* 15:20) also testifies to the deep faith inherent in Jewish women. The commentaries to this verse relate that as the women of the time prepared to leave Egypt, they were so confident that G-d would perform miracles on behalf of their people in the desert that they took drums with them so they could rejoice when the time came.

25. *Taanis* 31a.

26. *Pesachim* 119b.

for the feast celebrating the Redemption, everything has already been served, and we are sitting together with *Mashiach*. All that is necessary is that we open our eyes.[27]

The experience of such happiness demonstrates the strength of our trust in the promise of the Redemption, and the expression of this faith will, in turn, hasten its realization. And then,[28] "crowned with eternal happiness," we will proceed together[29] "with our youth and our elders..., with our sons and with our daughters," singing[30] "a new song for our Redemption and the deliverance of our souls."

27. See the essay entitled, "Open Your Eyes and See," in *Sound the Great Shofar*, pp. 109-114.
28. *Yeshayahu* 35:10.
29. *Shmos* 10:9.
30. The Pesach *Haggadah*; cf. *Mechilta, Beshalach* 15:1.

A Priestess in G-d's Sanctuary

SINAI AND SERVITUDE

It[1] was at Sinai, the fount of all *Yiddishkeit*, that G-d chose the Jews as His people, and gave them His Torah to serve as a guiding light through life — for them, and for all of creation — until the end of time. The revelation at Sinai also infused the Jewish people with the potential of refining the world through the Torah, preparing it to be a dwelling place for the *Shechinah*, the Divine Presence.

After this event is described in *Parshas Yisro*, the following weekly reading, *Parshas Mishpatim*, introduces the practical laws which govern the life of man, and which invest the corporeal world with spirituality.

This reading begins as follows:[2] "These are the laws that you shall set before [the Children of Israel]. If you buy a Jew-

---

1.   On *Shabbos Mevarchim* Adar I, 5746 [1986], the day on which *Parshas Mishpatim* was read, the Rebbe devoted one of his *sichos* to the current twelfth annual gathering of the alumni of Machon Chanah, an institute of higher learning for young women conducted in Crown Heights under the auspices of the *Chabad*-Lubavitch movement. Soon after, on *Motzaei Shabbos Parshas Vayakhel*, a Yiddish edition of this talk was issued in honor of the *Melaveh Malkah* of Machon Chanah. An English version based on that edition was later published in connection with the Week of the Jewish Woman, 1986.

2.   *Shmos* 21:1-2.

ish bondman, he shall serve for six years, but in the seventh year, he is to be set free without liability."

The institution of human servitude discussed in the Torah mirrors the divine service of man, as he refines his materiality and elevates the world around him by observing the Torah and its mitzvos:[3] "For the Children of Israel are servants unto Me." More particularly, the Zohar and the teachings of Chassidus distinguish three levels in the service of G-d, corresponding respectively to the three kinds of servant — the Canaanite bondman, the Jewish bondman, and the Jewish maidservant.

A HOME AWAY FROM HEAVEN

It is in the following weekly reading, Parshas Terumah, that G-d expresses His desire for a dwelling place on earth:[4] "They shall make Me a Sanctuary and I will dwell among them," indicating that the Tabernacle (the Mishkan) which the Jews were to build would create a "place" where the Shechinah could be manifest.

As we read week by week through Yisro, Mishpatim and Terumah (continuing on through Pekudei), with their respective leading themes — (a) the Giving of the Torah, (b) the enumeration of its laws to live by, and (c) the construction of the Mishkan — a definite progression becomes evident. First the requisite power is bestowed from above; then one begins to tackle his daily tasks like a dutiful bondman; and ultimately one finds that he has built a Sanctuary, the desired dwelling place on earth for one's Master in heaven.

---

3. Vayikra 25:55.
4. Ibid. 25:8.

More specifically: the Giving of the Torah represents education in Torah and *mitzvos*, which creates the framework within which one may attract the *Shechinah*; the servant state signifies diligence in our divine service; and the *Mishkan* represents the successful completion of all the efforts expended to transform the whole world (and our individual segments within it) into a dwelling place for G-d.

WOMEN AS ARCHITECTS & BUILDERS

In this vital mission of executing G-d's plan for the world, by transforming it into a home for Him, Jewish women and girls have been assigned a primary share. This explains why in every individual Jewish home — the counterpart and basic building-block of G-d's cosmic home — the homemaker is commonly referred to as *akeres habayis*,[5] the essence and foundation of the home, in material as well as in spiritual matters.

This precedence applies to all three aspects of divine service enumerated above.

(a) Regarding education (signified by the Giving of the Torah), it is obviously the mother who wields the greatest influence on her children from the youngest age; she is in fact responsible for the formative stages of their education.[6]

---

5.   Cf. *Tehillim* 113:9.
6.   Mothers have known this since the beginning of time. At the present time of year, as schools close for the summer, the resourcefulness of today's mothers is being challenged to the utmost. Many choose to invest some of the available free time in judicious storytelling. Others are able to communicate values, such as consideration for others, in the course of playing appropriate games. There are mothers who, while playing (say) Treasure Hunt with their children, will find ways of communicating the message that for a Jew, life is one big treasure hunt — explaining how a Jew must constantly search for hidden treasure, for the precious soul-gems hidden within himself and within every fellow Jew. (This was the message which the Baal Shem Tov

For this reason, every girl and especially every married woman has been endowed with the attributes needed to educate herself and others[7] — and foremost among these attributes is the innate feminine trait of gentleness. For the most elemental task of education, the implanting of values through the woman's natural warmth and love, must begin with[8] "the right hand that draws others near." Only then can the elimination of negative traits follow. After all, undesirable attributes are not an integral part of a Jew's true essence; they are merely superficial and temporary.

(b) In the area of basic life-work the *Gemara* asks,[9] "How does a woman help a man?" — and answers its own question by asking: "If a man brings home wheat does he chew it? If [he brings home] flax does he wear it? Does she not, then, bring light to his eyes and put him on his feet?" By converting the raw materials of the world into nourishing food and fitting garments, the Jewish wife and mother enables herself and her family to use materiality in the service of G-d. This form of servitude leads to her next role:

(c) The third area, the Tabernacle, is obviously the domain of the woman, for the spirit and atmosphere of the[10] "miniature sanctuary" — her home — are determined by the daily endeavors of its presiding priestess.

---

perceived in the verse (*Malachi* 3:12) in which G-d tells every individual Jew, "You shall be [for Me] a land of desire.")

7. This of course applies equally to those who are not involved in formal education. It is appropriate self-education that enables one to influence the attitudes that prevail in the home, in the schools, and in the wider environment.
8. *Sotah* 47a.
9. *Yevamos* 63a.
10. *Yechezkel* 11:16.

THE PRECEDENCE OF WOMEN

The Torah itself calls upon women to assume their leading roles in these three basic aspects of Judaism — Torah education, divine service, and the construction of a dwelling place for G-d:

(a) Before the Giving of the Torah, G-d directed Moshe to speak first to the women:[11] "This is what you shall say to the House of Yaakov, and tell the Israelites." The former phrase, *Rashi* explains, refers to the women; the latter, to the men. The women, then, were the first to receive the tidings of the preciousness of the Torah, and the directives on how to prepare themselves and their children to receive it.

(b) In the area of the servitude of Jewish bondmen, the category of divine service represented in the Torah by the Jewish maidservant (as explained below) is the highest.

(c) Describing the contributions brought to Moshe Rabbeinu for the construction of the *Mishkan*, the Torah writes,[12] "The men accompanied the women." Here, too, the women were followed by the men.[13]

The relationship between these three points is obvious: the women were first to receive the Torah and to offer their precious objects for the *Mishkan*, because they were also first in educating their children and in making each of their respective homes a *Mishkan*.

STAGES IN THE SOUL'S SERVITUDE

The *Zohar* sees the servitude of Jewish bondmen as an image for the descent of the divine soul into the physical

---

11. *Shmos* 19:3.
12. *Ibid.* 35:22.
13. Cf. *Rashi* and *Ramban, ad. loc.*

body and material world, with the purpose of becoming a servant or maidservant of the Creator. This it does by employing the Torah and its *mitzvos* to refine the body, the animal soul, and its own particular segment of the corporeal world. By doing this, the divine soul constructs a dwelling place for Divinity — and also, it should be added, it thereby becomes free.

As mentioned above, the *Kabbalah* goes on to explain that every individual has the potential for three successive stages of divine "servitude", which are represented in ascending order by the Canaanite bondman, the Jewish bondman, and the Jewish maidservant.[14]

When a person is taking his first steps in divine service, and is still at the level of the Canaanite bondman, his major task is to harness the instinctual drives of the animal soul that hankers after the worldly pleasures. This he accomplishes by standing in awe of his Master and accepting the yoke of His authority. At this stage, he bends the willful desires of his animal soul to conform in practice to the wishes of the Master.

When a person has graduated to the higher plane represented by the Jewish bondman, the attributes of the G-dly soul flood the animal soul with light; they empower the animal soul, too, to experience a certain degree of desire for G-dliness. Nevertheless, the individual's worldly desires have not been completely quashed or quieted. They still resemble the raw wheat and rough flax which must be refined and tempered before they are ready for human consumption.

At the highest level of divine service, as represented in the Torah by the Jewish maidservant, one's desires for worldly pleasures have been completely sublimated and transformed. One's only desire is to cleave to Divinity. At

---

14. In the original, *eved Kenaani*, *eved Ivri*, and *amah Ivriyah*, respectively.

this point one's role resembles that of the maidservant, who prepares food for human needs by refining and transforming raw substances into edible dainties. In the idiom of the *Zohar*,[15] the Jewish people "nourish their heavenly Father."

TO MARRY HER MASTER

In fact, however, the role represented by the Jewish maidservant takes the soul even further. The ultimate goal of this kind of servitude is that the maidservant marry her master; or, in the spiritual analog, that one leave the state of "maid" and become a "wife", and through this union draw the *Shechinah* into the world.

In the course of this upward odyssey, to borrow for a moment the terms of the *Kabbalah*, the soul ascends from the World of *Beriah* to the World of *Atzilus*, from the state of "maid" to the state of "bride", refining any physical impurities encountered along the way. In the ultimate consummation of this mystical marriage, the bride — *Knesses Yisrael*, the Congregation of Israel — is united with the Bridegroom, with the Holy One, blessed be He. And with this union, the Divine desire for a dwelling place in this world is fulfilled.

THE STATUS OF THE JEWISH MAIDSERVANT

The goal of this mystical marriage is reflected in the halachic particulars of the physical analogy.

In the first place, a Jewish girl may be bonded as a maidservant by her father only to a master with whom (or with whose son) a valid marriage can eventually be effected.[16]

---

15. *Zohar* III, 7b.
16. *Rambam, Mishneh Torah, Hilchos Avadim* 4:11.

Secondly, whereas in the case of a man,[17] "If he does not have the means he shall be sold [by the courts, as a bondman, to make restitution] for his theft," a Jewish girl may be bonded by her father as a maidservant for a certain period of time, only if he is in such dire straits that even the shirt on his back is borrowed. (And even then, the arrangement is valid only if the ultimate goal of marriage to the master can be envisaged at the outset, as explained above.)

In the spiritual analog, likewise: The soul is dispatched on its earthly journey into the body, only because the ultimate goal of union with G-d is envisaged from the outset, and only because of a pressing need — the establishment of G-d's home on earth.

It is in the kind of divine service represented by the Jewish maidservant, then, that the mission of the soul (and the soul's own simultaneous perfection) are clearly seen: This kind of divine service transforms the terrestrial world into a dwelling place for G-dliness; it converts the base attributes of the animal soul so that they desire only G-dliness; and ultimately, it attains a state of union with G-d.

SHORT-TERM AND LONG-RANGE GOALS

The ability to accomplish this finds its richest expression in the Jewish daughters of all generations — in all three major themes that figure in the Torah readings of this season, as enumerated earlier: in the transmission of the Torah, in the tempering of materiality so that it serves spiritual purposes, and in the consequent creation of a perfect dwelling place for G-d in the world (just as the womenfolk of an earlier generation were the first to act in the construction of the *Mishkan*).

---

17. *Shmos* 22:2.

However, over and beyond the noble mission of marrying and establishing a miniature sanctuary, discreetly guiding one's husband and children, and allowing one's living example to shine a ray of light into the lives of friends and acquaintances, something else remains. In addition to all the above, there remains the vital, long-range mission, of bringing about the ultimate and true Redemption by means of one's divine service.

Our Sages teach that[18] "It was by virtue of the righteous women of that generation that the Israelites were delivered from Egypt." So, too, must it be in our generation of[19] "the footsteps of *Mashiach*," a generation whose souls are a reincarnation of the souls of the generation of the Exodus.[20] And one thing is for sure: The women of this generation will not need a great deal of persuasion to leave the current state of *galus!*

THE OBLIGATIONS OF HUSBANDS

If Jewish women and girls are blessed with a role so elevated as that outlined above, Jewish men are obviously obliged by the Torah to show them the respect which is their due. Indeed, though his wife is his[21] "compatible helper," and is moreover dependent on him,[22] "The Sages likewise ordained that a man should honor his wife more than his own person"[23] — to show her honor and esteem, not equal to

---

18. *Sotah* 11b.
19. In the Aram. original, *ikvesa diMeshicha*, i.e., the generation that can hear the approaching footsteps of *Mashiach*; cf. *Sotah* 9:15, and *Rashi* there.
20. The *AriZal*, cited by R. Chaim Vital in *Shaar HaGilgulim*, Second Prelude.
21. *Bereishis* 2:18.
22. *Rambam, Mishneh Torah, Hilchos Ishus* 15:19.
23. This law obviously applies to a Jew who already has proper self-respect. We are taught, for example, that "A person has no authority whatever over his body — not to strike it, degrade it, or cause it pain in any way." (See the Alter Rebbe's *Shulchan Aruch, Hilchos Nizkei Guf VeNefesh*, sec. 4.) Like-

the respect he expects for himself, but far more. In plain words, he is obliged to help and respect and encourage his wife even more than he cares for himself. Thus, for example, if she requests his help in a matter which he considers to be insignificant, he ought to forego his own comfort and time and lend a hand.

When it comes to Torah and *mitzvos* — for example, when a wife wants to study Torah or *Chassidus*, or to go out to participate in outreach projects — it goes without saying that her husband must honor her desire (more than he would value his own), and give her every possible encouragement and assistance. There are ample precedents for the honor shown to Jewish women in the past for their achievements in Torah study, as related (for example) by the Rebbe Rayatz in his memoirs.

Certainly, the realm of women's Torah study and fulfillment of the *mitzvos* is clearly defined.[24] In the area of chassidic philosophy there are no limitations, for women are equally obligated to observe the ongoing commandments, such as loving G-d and fearing Him. Moreover, they bear an equal responsibility to disseminate the teachings of *Chassidus*.[25]

Preparing for a Cosmic Marriage

May G-d grant success to the activities and resolutions of this gathering, so that its participants will continue to carry out their true mission. In this way Jewish women and girls will hasten the arrival of the ultimate Redemption — the marriage of the entire Congregation of Israel with the Holy

---

wise, the *Rambam* (*Hilchos Rotzeach U'Shemiras Nefesh* 1:4) rules that a person's life is "the property of the Holy One, blessed be He."

24. See the Alter Rebbe's *Shulchan Aruch, Hilchos Talmud Torah*, sec. 1.
25. See the essay below entitled, "The Right to Know."

One, blessed be He.[26] At that time we will see the perfect revelation of G-d's dwelling place in the world, and the distinctive worth of women will be revealed. Indeed, at long last,[27] "Let there speedily be heard in the cities of Judah and in the courtyards of Jerusalem, the sound of joy and the sound of happiness, the sound of a groom and the sound of a bride" — in our time, and with gladness of heart.

---

26. Cf. *Shmos Rabbah*, sec. 15.
27. *Siddur Tehillat HaShem*, p. 410, paraphrasing *Yirmeyahu* 33:10-11.

Rights and Priorities

DISCRIMINATION?

A t[1] first glance, the call for equal rights is a persuasive one. Men and women alike are created[2] "in the image of G-d"; why should anyone be subject to unjust and unequal treatment? Yet Judaism, it is argued, discriminates against women both in lifestyle and in religious observance. While men have pursued their careers, women have traditionally kept the home and raised the children. And on the religious front, women are not called up for an *aliyah* to the congregational reading of the Torah, nor are they counted as part of a *minyan*. Does this constitute discrimination?

EQUAL BUT DIFFERENT

In the Divine plan for creation, men and women have distinct, diverse missions. These missions complement each

---

1. To mark the twentieth anniversary of the passing of his mother, the saintly *Rebbitzin* Chanah Schneerson, the Rebbe addressed a Crown Heights women's audience on 6 Tishrei, 5745 [1984].
2. *Bereishis* 1:27.

other, and together bring the Divine plan to harmonious fruition.[3]

The role of one is neither higher nor lower than the role of the other: they are simply different. And measuring from a certain perspective, the woman's tasks would rank higher, in terms both of self-fulfillment and of objective importance. For G-d in His infinite wisdom has granted the woman the ability to bring another Jew into the world, thereby securing the perpetuation of the[4] "holy people". He has entrusted her with the responsibility of raising her children in the ideals of our heritage, thereby securing the perpetuation of the Torah and its teachings, the word of G-d. And he has empowered her to be the mainstay of her entire household,[5] setting the tone for herself, her husband, and her children. Is there any mission worthier than this?

It is an unfortunate misconception of our times that this mission can be regarded condescendingly, as if inferior to earning money, or to any of the alternative life-goals proposed by society. Women have been given G-d's most precious gift, and they are being urged to exchange it for mere baubles.

PRIORITIES

If the cry for equal rights is aimed at persuading girls that they will be fulfilled only if they imitate men, it is misguided. To persuade a girl that she should first enter the business or

---

3. In the Torah, the words "male and female He created them" are immediately followed by the words, "And G-d blessed them" (*Bereishis* 1:27-28). On this juxtaposition the *Zohar* (I, 165a) comments that it is only when a man and a woman harmoniously fulfill their cosmic roles together as a married couple, that G-d's blessing fully rests upon them.

4. *Devarim* 7:6.

5. The phrase *akeres habayis*, borrowed from *Tehillim* 113:9, is popularly understood to mean "the mainstay of the household," from the root-word עיקר.

professional world and only afterwards, if she wants to, should she establish a family and a home, is to deprive her of her natural right. This set of priorities implies that raising children and running a warm and vibrant home is a secondary course of action, worth turning to only after one has first tackled something else. In the Torah view, to be a good mother and homemaker in itself needs solid preparatory study, as well as the firm conviction that this role is one's primary function.

This is not to say that for women to work is always wrong. It is more a matter of priorities, of knowing what is one's primary and Divinely-ordained role. Rather than being regarded as a goal in itself, a business or professional career can serve, for example, as an indirect means of upgrading the Torah atmosphere of the home. Indeed, there is a long Jewish tradition of women working to enable their husbands to devote themselves totally to studying Torah. Even then, of course, this has never been allowed to interfere with the primary role of raising a family.

SEPARATE PATHS

In a similar vein, the fact that women are not called up to the Torah for an *aliyah*[6] or are not counted as part of a *minyan*[7] is irrelevant to their worth. To demand such "rights" is simply to misunderstand what they mean.

---

6. *Shulchan Aruch, Orach Chaim* 282:3, citing *Megillah* 23a; the Alter Rebbe's *Shulchan Aruch, Orach Chaim* 282:5, and sources there.

   A wealth of primary halachic sources on this and on scores of related issues has been amassed and organized, in the original and in translation, in *Women and the Mitzvot*, Vol. I, which is entitled *Serving the Creator: A Guide to the Rabbinic Sources*, by Rabbi Getsel Ellinson.

7. *Beis Yosef* 55:a, citing the *Mordechai; Shulchan Aruch, Orach Chaim* 55:1, 4; the Alter Rebbe's *Shulchan Aruch, Orach Chaim* 55:5. See also *Mishpetei Uzziel*, Vol. II, on *Orach Chaim*, ch. 13.

Having an *aliyah* and being part of a *minyan* are indeed lofty matters. *Aliyah* literally means "ascent", referring both to the physical ascent up the steps to the platform where the Torah is read, and to the spiritual ascent that accompanies it. Through a *minyan*, G-d is sanctified both in this world and in all the spiritual worlds. But sanctity and spirituality are not man-made matters, to be toyed with at will. Holiness is attained by cleaving to G-d, and it is He who has established how one becomes sanctified and how one sanctifies.

There is not just one way in which to approach G-d: the Torah has prescribed different routes for men and for women. When two travelers arbitrarily exchange itineraries, neither arrives at his desired destination.

LIBERATION, NOT INDIGNITY

Ironically, the movement to liberate women can do the opposite: it can debase women. Liberation means being oneself. People who are sure of their own worth, secure in the conviction that they are equal to others, do not feel driven to imitate them. Having no reason to feel inferior to a man, a woman has no need to try to resemble a man. For a woman to adopt the lifestyle of a man is not only contrary to her nature and Divinely-given role, but betrays a lack of self-respect and self-esteem.

Just as diversity does not imply inequality, equality does not entail uniformity. Just as the Torah commands that[8] "A man shall not wear a woman's garment," so equally does it command that[8] "A man's garment shall not be upon a woman." This applies not only to the clothes we wear but also to the way we present ourselves. Neither men nor

---

8.   *Devarim* 22:5.

women carry out their G-d-given tasks or achieve self-fulfillment by imitating the other.

WHO DETERMINES A CHILD'S IDENTITY?

The blurring of the essential difference between man and woman is even robbing women of their basic rights as mothers. Jewish law affirms that a child belongs to the people of which his or her mother is a member, so that a child is Jewish only if the mother is Jewish.[9] One of the reasons for this is that the embryo is formed and nurtured in the mother's womb.

Flying in the face of this indisputable fact of nature, there are those who are currently proposing that the father should be the determining factor in establishing the child's identity. This is not only unreasonable, but in effect — as in child custody suits — robs the mother of the child whom she carried in her womb for nine months, for whom she went through the pain of childbirth, and whom she willingly brought into the world.

Women throughout the world, Jewish and non-Jewish, should protest strongly against this unjust distortion of the natural order. It is time to restore balance to a world where light is called darkness and darkness light.[10] Above all, it is time to restore to women the dignity of their sacred role as molders of young Jewish lives — when and where they are most needed.

---

9.   *Kiddushin* 68b on *Devarim* 7:4; *Kiddushin* 68a on *Shmos* 21:4.
10. Cf. *Yeshayahu* 5:20.

Part II:
Motherhood

Family Planning

DECISION-MAKING

To[1] our forebears, children were the greatest *nachas* possible, and the more children, the more *nachas*. The first *mitzvah* in the Torah is to[2] "be fruitful and multiply." To

---

1. In a series of addresses in 5740-41 [1980-81], the Rebbe discussed the assumptions underlying the arguments commonly advanced to justify family planning. The above essay is mainly a free summary of addresses delivered on the following occasions: *Shabbos Parshas Naso*, 5740 (see the essay entitled "The Torah Outlook on Family Planning" in *Sichos In English*, Vol. VI, p. 50ff.); the N'shei uBnos Chabad Convention, 17 Sivan, 5740 (see the essay entitled "Family Planning" in *Sichos In English*, Vol. VI, p. 79ff.); and *Shabbos Parshas Shlach*, 5740 (see *Sichos In English*, Vol. VI, p. 94).

    Soon after these addresses, sundry critics claimed that they were an unjustified "invasion of privacy," an offense against "freedom of choice," and in one case, "a violation of the Constitution" (!). The closing section of the above essay, beginning with the subheading "Freedom of Choice," is a free adaptation of part of the Rebbe's response to these critics on *Shabbos Parshas Korach*, 5740 (see the essay entitled "Free Choice and Responsibility" in *Sichos In English*, Vol. VI, pp. 103-106).

    The Rebbe again spoke on this subject on Rosh Chodesh Shvat, 5741 (see the essay entitled "Family Planning" in *Sichos In English*, Vol. VIII, p. 179ff.).

2. *Bereishis* 1:28. The fact that procreation is the first *mitzvah* in the Torah indicates its primary importance. According to Scriptural law, a father has fulfilled this command once he has brought at least one son and one daughter into the world. Nevertheless, even after this *mitzvah* is fulfilled, there remains a Rabbinic command to continue having children. (See *Rambam*,

bring up children, to initiate them into the faith of their fathers and mothers, to educate them in the Torah and the *mitzvos*, — this is the true *nachas* that has always been eagerly treasured by our people.

Today, in many quarters, this approach is being challenged. With well-meaning concern, couples are being urged to plot out the size of their families in advance, so that the time of their children's conception be anticipated and adequately prepared for.

It must be clearly stated at the outset that according to the *Halachah*, Jewish law, the use of contraception is a matter which requires Rabbinic consultation. Some methods are unequivocally prohibited. Other means are permitted, but only in special circumstances, and only after consultation with competent halachic authorities.

Though compliance with the *Halachah* overrules human reason, in this case the two are consonant; common experience attests to the wisdom of the Torah approach. Our Torah tradition has nurtured families which have built homes filled with care, communication, and satisfying inner purpose, raising children who are prepared to accept their roles in society with joy and responsibility.[3]

THE THIRD PARTNER

What lies at the heart of the Torah approach? — The conception that faith in G-d is not restricted merely to the

---

Mishneh Torah, Hilchos Ishus 15:1, 4, 16; Shulchan Aruch, Even HaEzer, sec. 1.)

3. For a comprehensive analysis of the social and nationwide obligations involved, such as the total Jewish birthrate, the needs of the Jewish community, and the like, see the article by Rabbi Z. Posner entitled "By Whatever Means...," in The Modern Jewish Woman: A Unique Perspective (Lubavitch Educational Foundation for Jewish Marriage Enrichment, N.Y., 1981).

synagogue, but embraces every aspect of our existence. And there is no area in which this is so evident as having children. Man cannot create life; no power on earth can guarantee the birth of a baby. The key to that decision[4] is in the hands of G-d alone. He is the third Partner in the conception of every child.[5]

Any concerns and reservations that a couple may have, the third Partner understands too; He also knows what potentials they have to cope with those concerns. He is gracious and merciful, and will grant children only when there is the potential for them to lead a life with meaning and purpose.

Besides, when a partnership is offered and rejected, a second offer may not be forthcoming so rapidly. Couples who have spurned the potential blessing of life which G-d offered them in their younger years may not be granted it later on. A couple should accept G-d's blessings when He offers them, gratefully. Let them rest assured that the third Partner, being benevolent and all-knowing, can be trusted to know what time is the best time.

MANAGING G-D'S ACCOUNTS

Faith in the third Partner's planning also resolves one of the commonest justifications offered for family planning — the fear of being unable to support more than a certain proposed number of children. Naturally, parents want the best for their children, and this entails accepting a financial burden. But being a good provider is not determined by one's own efforts alone.[6] True, the Torah requires that a man work

---

4. *Taanis* 2a.
5. *Kiddushin* 30b.
6. We are warned against such a delusion in the verse, "My strength and the power of my hand have made me all this prosperity" (*Devarim* 8:17).

to provide for his family. But it is a primary tenet of Judaism that all success and all wealth comes from G-d, that it is His blessings that give sustenance,[7] not one's own unaided efforts. He will provide for all the children He gives to a couple:[8] "He Who gives life gives food."

Couples who undertake financial responsibilities beyond their immediate capacities, and find it quite natural and reasonable to depend on family and friends to help them get married and set up their home, should certainly find it natural and reasonable to depend on Him of Whom it is written,[9] "The silver is Mine, the gold is Mine." G-d's accounting system is not our worry; everyone will receive what he needs. It is He Who provides for all of His creatures; one mouth more will not overburden Him.

THE TOLL VS. THE NACHAS

A candid appraisal of one's priorities raises some challenging questions: What does one really want out of life, and what is one doing to get it? Is it possible that luxuries have been mistaken for necessities? Perhaps the real sources of happiness and well-being, those which don't cost a penny, have been bartered for costlier, but less reliable sources of satisfaction?

Defining one's priorities resolves another common and serious concern of potential parents: the personal toll that raising children exacts — a burden in terms of energy, time, and freedom of movement, not to mention the emotional investment required. As with the above-mentioned financial issue, however, the real question here is not one of insuffi-

7. Cf. "It is the blessing of G-d that bestows wealth" (*Mishlei* 10:22).
8. Popular Aram. adage, based on a teaching of R. Shmuel bar Nachmani in *Taanis* 8b.
9. *Chagai* 2:8.

cient personal resources, but rather one of priorities. In many other areas of life, such as careers and other personal goals, people choose to put up with prolonged inconvenience and even sacrifice in order to attain their object — if it is considered important enough.

For a person who considers the pursuit of immediate enjoyment a major goal in life, children can no doubt prove to be an obstacle. But a person whose concept of satisfaction centers on meaning and depth will see children as a genuine source of joy, which mellows and grows with the years as they mature and develop, and ultimately raise families of their own.

The challenge is the scope of one's foresight and planning: Is it long-term or short-term oriented? A person who considers not only the present, but looks ahead to the future, will realize that the pleasure of a few years of freedom from the encumbrance of children soon dissipates, and their shortsightedness has deprived them of the ongoing satisfaction and comfort of children and grandchildren. Is that looking too far ahead? — No more than those who look ahead twenty years or more worrying about their future ability to bring up and educate children.

AN ALTRUISTIC ARGUMENT

An honest definition of one's own priorities also answers the altruistic objection put forward by women who would like to have more time to devote to worthy causes and good works. Now charitable causes are undoubtedly worthy pursuits, but no less worthy is child-raising. Who has determined that charity is superior to rearing children? — Certainly not the Torah. A child granted by G-d indicates by his very presence what must take precedence.

Furthermore, all of our endeavors require G-d's blessing for success. As many a happy mother will testify, the charitable endeavors which she undertakes in the limited time available to her, are blessed with more than enough success to compensate for the time spent in raising a child. Besides, who can know what great things that child, raised with the loving care of his parents, will ultimately achieve?

For an explicit lesson in priorities, one need only read the plain text that narrates the story of the birth of the prophet Samuel.[10] The mother of this child was the prophetess Chanah, so one can imagine what sublime experiences of spiritual enlightenment awaited her on each of her annual visits to the *Mishkan* at Shiloh. And these were not merely her private concern: she shared her individual enlightenment with our people as a whole. Nevertheless, once Shmuel was born, she chose for a time to forego that bliss in favor of a loftier mission — until she had gently nurtured her baby into boyhood.

UNDESIRABLE EFFECTS

Dwarfing all the theoretical arguments and counter-arguments, the statistics of daily experience reveal some sobering facts. Family planning has often been advocated as a buttress to make the family structure sturdier. Yet precisely in the past few generations, when the concept of family planning has become so widespread, we see the highest incidence of marital discord, domestic tension, misguided parenting, separations, divorces, nervous frustration, and psychiatric disorders.

The human body and psyche were created with infinite intricacy; disrupting their natural functions inevitably invites

---

10. *I Shmuel*, ch. 1 (and note verses 22-24).

aberrations. Little wonder, then, that professional marriage counselors are increasingly blaming the tensions set up by birth control for a wide range of marital, mental and emotional breakdowns.[11]

In earlier generations, especially in Jewish homes, where family planning was never considered, the divorce rate was infinitesimal. The prevalent respect and harmony between Jewish husband and wife were legendary in the eyes of the world. And the most critical corollary of this is too obvious to need mentioning — the inevitable effect on the mental and physical health of children who grow up in a peaceful and harmonious household with shared ideals and values.

A LIGHT TO THE NATIONS

What has been said above about birth control applies not only to Jews, but to non-Jews as well. All people are created so that the world will be populated and not left barren:[12] "He did not create it a waste land: He formed it to be inhabited." In a personal sense, too, having children brings settled purpose to one's life.

We have a responsibility to contribute to society at large by spreading an awareness of the principles and values that will enable all men to lead normal lives, in tune with their inner nature.[13] Beyond the limited sphere of our friends and acquaintances, we must convince the leaders of the country to fight against family planning and birth prevention by lob-

---

11. To revert, parenthetically, to the financial argument: The substantial sums commonly invested in psychiatrists and sundry experts, could well have been put to healthier uses.
12. *Yeshayahu* 45:18.
13. See *Rambam, Mishneh Torah, Hilchos Melachim* 8:10, on the obligation to teach non-Jews the Seven Universal Laws commanded to Noach and his descendants. By extension, this includes sharing the values and principles needed for the development of a wholesome society.

bying in Congress, simply, soberly, and with common sense. The elected officials are normal people who will understand a normal explanation. They have the potential to create and encourage programs that will stimulate a greater understanding of the importance of raising families and enhance the prestige of such endeavors.

FREEDOM OF CHOICE

Calling for such programs has been protested as an invasion of privacy. The proper province of governmental concern, it is argued, extends as far as national security and economics, but not personal decisions such as having children.

As civilizations develop, however, we find governments assuming certain responsibilities for their citizens, even if doing so appears to limit their free choice. In the United States, for example, a great deal of money is spent to maintain a Federal agency known as the Food and Drug Administration, which tests products to ensure that they are fit for human consumption. A product which is proved to be dangerous is not permitted on the public market; the manufacturers are legally prosecuted if they persist in its distribution; if there is a possibility of harmful side-effects, a product must be accompanied by a warning on the label.

One might question the right of any government to limit the products its citizens are permitted to consume. It is obvious that some forms of social legislation are necessary, for in its absence,[14] "Men would swallow one another alive." But isn't one's ingestion of food and drugs a purely personal matter? Nevertheless, a government that is truly concerned about its citizens will do everything it possibly can to keep them from harm, even harm which they choose to inflict

---

14. *Avos* 3:2.

upon themselves. And therefore that agency has been set up and continues to function.

This is demonstrated most graphically by a more radical example: society's response to an attempted suicide. If someone wishes to throw himself from a bridge, police and coast guard are mobilized. No matter how aged he may be, the government will expend immense resources of time, money, and equipment to prevent him from cutting his life short. It is not only an individual's desire to harm another which society finds intolerable, but the desire to harm himself as well.

PUBLIC EDUCATION

Here, however, we are dealing not with law enforcement, but simply with an education towards values. The public resources that are being spent today to foster family planning should be put to positive use — to cultivate a widespread appreciation of the meaning of family, of what it means to raise and care for children. The time-tested values of the Torah need to be translated into the vernacular and spread throughout society at large. For this purpose, research is also necessary. The tools of social science should be employed to clearly demonstrate that the Torah's approach provides man with the environment best suited for meaningful and satisfying life experience.

It has been said that today there is no such thing as an *apikores:* there is only the *am haaretz*.[15] Opposition — whether in the area of family planning, or, more broadly, in the area of *taharas hamishpachah*, the laws securing family purity — is rooted in ignorance; it is based on the misconception that the way of Torah runs contrary to a natural way of

---

15. The former term means "atheist"; the latter term, "ignoramus". In other words, to qualify as a responsible disbeliever one must first be equipped with a sound knowledge of what one claims to reject.

life. When people are educated to appreciate the simple truth, that the Torah leads us to harmony with who we are and what our real purpose is in this world, their opposition will cease.

BEYOND MORTAL GRASP

The effects of birth control are more world-shaking than any mortal can appreciate. For every Jew and every Jewish child is[16] "an entire world." Indeed, our Sages teach[17] that even if one single Jew had been absent from Mt. Sinai, the Torah could not have been given. They teach, moreover,[18] that *Mashiach* will not come until all the possible souls are born into this world.

Considering this, can any man with his limited understanding presume to grasp the possible consequences of preventing a particular Jew from being born?

THE MATRIARCHS AS MOTHERS

We are all descendants of the four Matriarchs of our people — Sarah, Rivkah, Rachel and Leah. Though each was distinguished for her particular gifts, there was one common bond between them: each longed for children, with a yearning that knew no limits. The Torah, usually so sparing of its words, describes in detail the lengths to which they went to achieve this end.

They were the archetypes of all Jewish women, and we would do well to heed their lesson. True self-worth does not belong to those who blindly follow the consensus dictated by contemporary society. Children, many children, are the

---

16. *Sanhedrin* 37a.
17. *Mechilta, Shmos* 19:11; *Devarim Rabbah* 7:8.
18. *Yevamos* 62a.

greatest gift and blessing that G-d can bestow upon us; imagined obstacles should not be allowed to stand in the way of enjoying these blessings. And then, with these blessings,[19] "with our youth and our elders..., with our sons and our daughters," we will go out joyfully to greet our righteous Redeemer, speedily, in our own times.

---

19. *Shmos* 10:9.

Three Mothers

THE HAND THAT ROCKS THE CRADLE

Rosh HaShanah[1] is a day of judgment and prayer, and also a day when prayers are answered. Our Sages relate that[2] "Sarah, Rachel and Chanah were all granted children on Rosh HaShanah." Each of these three great women was possessed by an ardent desire: to bring a Jewish child into the world. With dedicated determination, they turned to G-d in sincere prayer that they be granted this privilege.

A mother's joy is not merely in giving birth to a child, but in raising him and nurturing his growth. The three women mentioned above exemplify how a Jewish mother should devote herself to her children's development from infancy to adulthood.

For education is a commitment that begins from the cradle — and indeed from conception.[3] This concept, which has

1. This essay is based on a *farbrengen* held by the Rebbe on 6 Tishrei, 5741 [1980], to mark the anniversary of the passing of his late revered mother, *Rebbitzin* Chanah Schneerson ע״ה.
2. *Berachos* 29a.
3. Our Sages counsel certain restrictions in diet and conduct during pregnancy, because of their effects on the child after birth. (See *Rus Rabbah* 3:13; *Talmud Yerushalmi, Chagigah* 2:1; *Chagigah* 15a, *Tosafos s.v. Shuvu.*)

been popularized by secular culture only recently, has been the intellectual and actual heritage of Jewish mothers since ancient times.

FIRST IMPRESSIONS

In generations past, our grandmothers used to fondly affix Biblical verses to the cradles of their infants, so that their first sight in this world would be the holy letters of the Torah.[4] The lullabies with which they sang their little ones to sleep were homely Yiddish verses in praise of "*Toireh, di beste sechoireh*" ("Torah, the choicest merchandise"), which was described in rhyme as being sweeter even than the toddler's familiar delicacies such as "*rozhinkes mit mandlen*" ("raisins and almonds").[5]

---

4. At the *farbrengen* of *Yud-Tes* Kislev, 5747 [1986], the Rebbe recalled the age-old custom of hanging up appropriate inscriptions, from the onset of labor, for the protection of mother and child. (Sources for the custom may be found in *Sefer Raziel HaMalach, Tishbi, Eidus LeYisrael, Keser Shem Tov* (ed. Gagin), and *Segulos Yisrael.*) Because these texts traditionally include Psalm 121, whose theme is simple trust in G-d's protective presence, its opening words *(Shir HaMaalos)* gave these inscriptions their name. In addition, such inscriptions often include other Biblical verses, Divine Names, and names of angels. In some communities the custom takes the form of an amulet worn by the mother. In any case, "An accepted Jewish custom assumes the force of Torah" (cf. *Tosafos* on *Menachos* 20b, *s.v. Nifsal.*)

    The Rebbe pointed out that now that childbirth generally takes place in hospitals, this traditional practice should be renewed there, both in the labor ward (cf. *Berachos* 54b on the need for vigilance there), and, if possible, on the baby's cradle. The Rebbe suggested that conscientious doctors would appreciate that the resultant peace of mind would benefit their patients as well as themselves, and they would thus be readily persuaded to cooperate in reinstituting the practice in hospitals, even in outlying centers with small Jewish populations.

    The above talk of the Rebbe was originally adapted and published as an essay entitled "*Mazel-Tov*: A Blessing for Mother and Child" in *Sichos In English*, Vol. XXXIV, p. 1ff.

5. Of course children should be given incentives on their own level to study Torah and to conduct themselves as they should. As they mature, however,

Looking back for earlier precedents, we find that when Rabban Yochanan ben Zakkai enumerated the exalted qualities of his greatest disciples, he surprisingly praised R. Yehoshua ben Chananyah with the words,[6] "Happy is she who bore him." This was of course a praise, not of R. Yehoshua himself, but of his mother, for in fact he owed his greatness to her. From his earliest infancy she would carry his cradle to the local House of Study, so that from the very beginning his ears would be sensitized to the harmonies hidden in the words of the Torah.[7] And it was those crucial first impressions which quietly laid the unseen but deep foundations for his future greatness.

GROWING OUT OF THE CRADLE

As infants grow into toddlers, their education begins to separate out into different paths. The wisest of men counseled,[8] "Educate a child according to his way; even when he grows older, he will not depart from it." Every child has "his way," a unique tendency and nature of his own. A wise mother, observing how each of her budding twigs reaches out and unfolds and grows towards the light in its own individual way, refrains from pruning and pushing and imposing a uniform style on them all. Respecting their uniqueness, she cultivates their individual gifts.[9]

---

they should be gently weaned from appreciating only the sweetness of *rozhinkes mit mandlen*, to appreciating the sweetness of the Torah and its *mitzvos*.
6. *Avos* 2:9.
7. *Talmud Yerushalmi, Yevamos* 1:6.
8. *Mishlei* 22:6.
9. In the above-quoted *mishnah* (*Avos* 2:9), Rabban Yochanan ben Zakkai enumerated the praiseworthy qualities of his five outstanding disciples, thus encouraging them to flourish in all their diversity. See *In the Paths of Our Fathers* (Kehot; N.Y., 1994), p. 53, for the comment of the Rebbe on this *mishnah*.

This was the attitude of our Matriarchs, Sarah and Rachel. Their sons, Yitzchak and Yosef, were very different, both in their spiritual personalities and in the missions they were assigned in the world at large.

YITZCHAK: A LIFE OF TRANQUILLITY

The uniqueness of Sarah's vision for Yitzchak's growth can be seen by comparison with the approach of her husband. Avraham Avinu, in his gentle compliance, would have been satisfied with Yishmael as G-d's gift of a son in his old age:[10] "If only Yishmael might live before You." Sarah, however, continued to pray for a child born of her own flesh and blood, whom she would raise to be the progenitor of the Jewish people. As G-d Himself later told Avraham,[11] "in Yitzchak will your children be called": only from him would the Jewish people descend.

Later on, once Yitzchak was born, she continuously strove to safeguard his Jewish upbringing, demanding that Yishmael be removed from his company:[12] "Drive away this maidservant and her son." Though Avraham was troubled by Sarah's unexpected sternness,[13] G-d vindicated her approach:[14] "Whatever Sarah tells you, listen to her voice." It was thus her uncompromising dedication to her son's Jewish upbringing that resulted in his courageous willingness to offer up his life as a sacrifice to G-d in the test of the *Akeidah*,[15] the Binding of Yitzchak.

---

10. *Bereishis* 17:18.
11. *Ibid.* 21:12.
12. *Ibid.* 21:10.
13. *Ibid.* 21:11.
14. *Ibid.* 21:12. As paraphrased by *Rashi*, "Listen to the voice of the Divine Spirit within her."
15. *Ibid.* 22:1-19.

His mother's early training continued to guide Yitzchak throughout his later life, too, as[16] "a perfect sacrifice," a man whose entire life was an offering to G-d. As such, he never left the Holy Land[17] — "the land that G-d's eyes rest upon from the beginning of the year to the end of the year."[18] Now the Holy Land is the first to receive G-d's blessings, and through it they flow to other lands.[19] As a result, Yitzchak was so wealthy that people would say, "Rather the waste of Yitzchak's mules than the silver and gold of [King] Avimelech."[20] His life was thus not only free of the discomforts of exile which his father Avraham and his son Yaakov experienced, but also singularly free of material worry. Yet in all this environment of prosperity, he lived his life in unswerving fear of G-d. This was reflected in his digging of wells in search of subterranean springs,[21] a physical activity which parallels the spiritual labor of digging into one's core, and revealing one's inner G-dly essence.[22]

YOSEF: A LIFE OF STRUGGLE

Rachel raised her son Yosef in an utterly different environment. He was born in Charan,[23] "the target of G-d's fury in the world," in the deceitful household of his maternal grandfather, Lavan. Nevertheless, his mother's dedication to his upbringing empowered him to withstand the challenges of a life of struggle.

---

16. *Rashi* on *Bereishis* 26:2, based on *Bereishis Rabbah* 64:3.
17. *Bereishis* 26:2-3.
18. *Devarim* 11:12.
19. *Sifri, Devarim*, sec. 40; *Ramban* on *Devarim* 11:12.
20. *Rashi* on *Bereishis* 26:13, based on *Midrash Rabbah*.
21. *Bereishis* 26:18ff.
22. *Torah Or, Parshas Toldos*, p. 17c.
23. Cf. *Rashi* on *Bereishis* 11:32; in the original, playing on the Hebrew place-name Charan, *charon-af shel [Makom ba]-olam*.

Unlike his paternal grandfather, Yitzchak, Yosef lived in *Eretz Yisrael* only up to the age of seventeen, when he was sold by his brothers. Thereafter, he spent his entire adult life in Egypt,[24] "the depravity of the earth."[25] He was forced to suffer for years as a slave and prisoner. Even when he rose to the station of viceroy, his duties occupied most of his time, keeping him from direct involvement in spiritual pursuits. And even then, he was still subject to the final authority of Pharaoh:[26] "I will make the throne higher than you."

Yet despite his most unpromising environment, Yosef lived a life of such integrity that he is remembered as Yosef HaTzaddik — thanks to the early training which his mother invested in him.

A JEW FOR ALL SEASONS

There are times in the life of every Jew, child or adult, which parallel the two utterly different conditions of life represented by Yitzchak and Yosef.

From Yitzchak we can learn how his material prosperity never cooled his ardent devotion to G-d. On the contrary, the courage and submission which he demonstrated at the *Akeidah* remained with him for the rest of his life.

From Yosef we can learn how material obstacles did not dampen his spirits. On the contrary, his suffering in fact led to his future role as viceroy of Egypt. There are times when we, too, can likewise take heart and be encouraged to stand firm until events take a turn for the better. Though we remain subject to the law of "Pharaoh", to the limitations of our environment, we can still utilize it for the service of G-d.

---

24. *Bereishis* 42:12.
25. Even after he passed away, it was well over a hundred years before his remains were returned to *Eretz Yisrael*.
26. *Bereishis* 41:40.

TOILING TOWARD THE REDEMPTION

The third great woman who was granted a child on Rosh HaShanah was Chanah. Exultant with gratitude to G-d after the birth of her son Shmuel, she uttered a prophecy[27] which alludes to the tribulations that the Jews would suffer in exile, and to the ultimate coming of *Mashiach*.[28] Just as her name derives from the Hebrew word *chein* ("grace" or "charm"), a quality that transcends the finite categories of human reason, so too her prophecy speaks of the transcendent spiritual revelations of the era of *Mashiach*.

Like Chanah, we too, despite the difficulties of exile, can attain a higher plane of spiritual endeavor, by concentrated toil in our Torah study. As the *Zohar* explains,[29] exile need not be experienced in terms of physical hardship, but rather through exerting one's energies in the "toil of the Torah." And indeed, this endeavor brings the long-promised Redemption one step closer.

RACHEL'S CHILDREN RETURN

When *Mashiach* finally arrives in the imminent world-wide Redemption, we will be led back to *Eretz Yisrael* by way of Rachel's tomb, just as our forefathers passed by it on their way to exile in Babylonia.[30] Then, on their way into exile, it was the soul of Rachel which interceded for them and gave them encouragement. And, in the future Redemption, as we

27. *I Shmuel* 2:1-10.
28. On other occasions the Rebbe has pointed out the direct connection between bringing children into the world, and the hastening of the Redemption, as follows. In *Yevamos* 62a, the *Gemara* mentions the heavenly treasure house called *Guf*, where every unborn soul awaits its descent into a newborn body. The *Gemara* there teaches: "The son of David (i.e., *Mashiach*) will not come before *Guf* will have been emptied of all its souls."
29. *Zohar* I, 27a; III, 153a.
30. See *Rashi* on *Bereishis* 48:7.

emerge out of exile, it will again be Rachel who will encourage us, and take pride in the fact that all her children are coming home.

Moreover, as G-d's children are gathered in from the Diaspora, so too, *with* their return, G-d Himself will return (so to speak) from the exile of His Divine Presence.[31] He will guide every Jew[32] "by the hand" out of exile, and lead him home — to a Holy Land *complete* in all its boundaries as specified by the Torah, as part of a Jewish people *complete* in the definition of its national identity, and *complete* in its uncompromising observance of the entire Torah.[33]

---

31. See the end of ch. 6 of the Alter Rebbe's *Iggeres HaTeshuvah* (in *Lessons In Tanya*, Vol. III, pp. 1067-8), which explains this teaching of the Sages (*Megillah* 29a; *Sifri, Masei* 35:4) on *Devarim* 30:3.

32. *Rashi* on *Devarim* 30:3.

33. In the original, the three key phrases here are: *shleimus haaretz, shleimus haam, shleimus haTorah.*

Part III:
Study & Observance

The Right to Know

CHANGING ROLES: CHANGING QUESTIONS

Alert[1] to the far-reaching role changes taking place around herself and within her own life, many a woman today is asking: "What is my place in Torah?" "Are there limits to the Torah subjects I should study?"

To begin at the beginning: When G-d first told Moshe to prepare the Jews to receive the Torah, He commanded him,[2] "This is what you shall say to the House of Yaakov and speak to the Children of Israel." Our Sages explain[3] that "the House of Yaakov" refers to Jewish women, and "the Children of Israel," to the men; i.e., G-d told Moshe to approach the women first.

This order implies a sense of priority: for the Torah to be perpetuated among the Jewish people, precedence must be given to Jewish women. This statement may appear questionable in view of several traditional attitudes. These atti-

---

1. The above essay is compounded from the account (published in *Hisvaaduyos*) of the *yechidus* which the Belzer Rebbe had with the Rebbe on the 4th of Adar II, 5741 [1981], as well as from talks delivered by the Rebbe on other occasions.
2. *Shmos* 19:3.
3. *Mechilta*, cited by *Rashi* on the above verse.

tudes, however, need to be examined by the objective standard of Torah law as applied to the Torah requirements of contemporary society.

THE PRACTICAL AND THE MYSTICAL DIMENSIONS

For a start, the *Halachah* (Torah law)[4] requires a woman to study all the laws and concepts needed to enable her to observe the *mitzvos* which she is obligated to fulfill. This encompasses a vast and varied curriculum, including the intricate laws of (for example): *Shabbos, kashrus,* and *taharas hamishpachah* (family purity); all the positive *mitzvos* that are not contingent on a specific time; and virtually all the prohibitive *mitzvos*, whether of Scriptural or Rabbinic authority. Indeed, many learned men would be happy if their Torah knowledge would be as complete.

Nevertheless, even those who do concede to the above curriculum for women often draw a line between (a) instruction in the bare *Dos* and *Don'ts*, and (b) "too much" education — such alleged luxuries, for example, as guidance towards a satisfying philosophy of life; an appreciation of the dynamics set in motion by the observance of a *mitzvah;* an understanding of how a Jew connects with 'his Creator by studying His Torah; and an informed sensitivity to the way in which all Jews are part of the same spiritual anatomy.

Indisputably, however, included among the many *mitzvos* which a woman is fully obligated to observe are the cardinal commandments of knowing G-d, loving Him, fearing Him, and the like. (Indeed, these *mitzvos*[5] "devolve upon us as a constant obligation, never ceasing [for either a man or a woman] for even a moment throughout his life.") Obviously,

---

4. *Tur Shulchan Aruch, Yoreh Deah* 246:6; *Sefer Chassidim,* sec. 313; the Alter Rebbe's *Shulchan Aruch, Hilchos Talmud Torah* 1:14.
5. See the introductory letter to *Sefer HaChinuch.*

one cannot wholeheartedly fulfill these ongoing obligations without a mastery of certain spiritual concepts. This is clearly spelled out in the verse,[6] "*Know* the G-d of your fathers and serve Him with a full heart." In order to attain this *knowledge*, as well as all the above manifestations of informed sensitivity, both men and women need to study *pnimiyus haTorah*, the Torah's mystic dimension. And this dimension is articulated and accessible in the teachings of *Chassidus*.[7]

For similar reasons, women would do well to focus their attention on the Aggadic aspects of the Torah as assembled in *Ein Yaakov*, since our Sages have noted the powerful impact of such study in cultivating one's spiritual emotions.[8]

PRECEDENTS AND PROGRESS

Throughout the generations, there have been accounts of particular women with immense Torah knowledge. The *Talmud*[9] mentions Beruriah, the daughter of R. Chaninah ben Teradyon and the wife of R. Meir. Throughout the Middle Ages, we find records of many women who proofread

---

6. *I Divrei HaYamim* 28:9.
7. See *Sefer HaMinhagim: The Book of Chabad-Lubavitch Customs* (English translation; Kehot, N.Y., 1992), pp. 192-194, where the detailed discussion of this subject by the Rebbe concludes with the following note: "...Keeping all this in mind, it is self-evident that women too are obliged to study that dimension of the Torah which engenders and gives birth to a love and awe of the Almighty, explaining how His unity is utterly unique, and so on. For it is with regard to every single Jew and Jewess that the Torah writes (*Devarim* 30:14), 'For this thing is very near to you, in your mouth and in your heart, that you may do it.' "

The sources which the Rebbe cites in the above-mentioned work are traced in an in-depth study (in Hebrew) by R. Avraham Baruch Pevsner entitled *"Limud Torah SheBe'al-Peh LeNashim,"* in *Sefer HaYovel: Karnos Tzaddik* (Kehot; Kfar Chabad, 5752), p. 661.
8. Cf.: "Do you seek to know Him Who spoke and the world came into being? — Study *Aggadah!*" (*Sifri, Eikev*, 49:11, 22).
9. *Pesachim* 62b.

and corrected their husbands' learned Torah discourses.[10] In his memoirs, the Rebbe Rayatz describes how the Alter Rebbe's family exemplified the ideal of advanced Torah scholarship for women, and the Rebbe Rayatz himself educated his own daughters in this spirit.

As a departure from this situation, where advanced learning was reserved for the privileged few, recent generations have witnessed the foundation of schools and institutions for the many. Previously, in the spirit of the principle that[11] "All the glory of the king's daughter is inward," girls and young women would be educated by their parents and grandparents at home. Yet even when sociological conditions changed and young girls left the protective and supportive home environment, the first devoutly observant schools established for them faced well-meaning but vehement opposition. With time, however, recognizing the possible inroads which an open secular society could make, the initial opposition to the daring novelty soon fell away.

A Responsible Response to Native Curiosity

Today, this entire issue is no longer a debatable academic question. It is a fact of life that children and young people today ask questions and expect satisfying answers. Whatever questions they may not have initiated spontaneously, they are exposed to by the media or by their peers. In the secular studies taught at most Jewish schools, students are taught to probe, to question, to seek the reasons behind the facts.

The conclusion is simple: If children are seeking the rationale for what they are being taught in the world of *Yiddishkeit*, we must supply them with informed and authoritative answers. If not, answers will most certainly be sought

---

10. *Igros Kodesh* (Letters) of the Rebbe Rayatz, Vol. V, p. 336.
11. *Tehillim* 45:14.

elsewhere. It is neither wise nor possible to stifle a naturally curious mind. On the contrary: the answers to the key questions about a Jew's life in this world — his Torah study, his *mitzvah* observance, his daily prayers, his interpersonal relations — are the staple diet needed to nourish and nurture the budding and groping inner life of every Jewish child.

For a simple example of this need: Suppose a young girl is faced on the one hand with the self-styled certainties presented by her science teacher, impressively buttressed by facts and explanations, and on the other hand, with the evasiveness of her religious teachers. Any resultant doubts can even affect the level of her actual observance for a lifetime.

Certainly it would be a fine thing if all secular subjects in religious schools were taught in accordance with the Torah view. But as things stand, the law of the land in many countries prescribes that the secular text books used must be approved by the education authorities. Various remedies have been tried to cope with the excess baggage in these textbooks. Offending pages have been removed, partially photostated copies have been put together, and so on. But these are all piecemeal solutions, and the time needed to implement the more lasting measures would jettison an entire generation. In the meantime, then, students should be told unequivocally that any theory which contradicts the Torah is false. At the same time, clear and informed answers are required, and only then will a child's thirst for knowledge be sated.

Though the need to educate boys comprehensively is equally urgent, girls should receive a special emphasis, for as future mothers they will be chiefly responsible for the upbringing of their children, especially in the formative years. It is to them that their young children will run with questions from school, and it is they who must be intellectually equipped to guide their little ones in the right path.

All Children are Our Children

There is a related area in which educators would do well to cultivate a responsive awareness to sociological change — and that is, the observance of the laws of family purity. Yet many rabbis consistently refuse to address their congregants on this most vital of subjects, because of a misplaced sense of modesty. It has sometimes been argued that with "our" children, there is no need to offset misinformed or unwholesome attitudes by appropriate instruction from the Torah of life. But *all* Jewish children are "our" children, and we must worry about them as much as our own.

Changing Questions: Changing Answers

There are those who even today oppose higher formal education for girls, on the grounds that it is not part of the legacy sanctified through centuries of usage by our pious forebears. The traditions of our fathers are indeed holy, but new problems demand fresh approaches. There are many phenomena universally accepted today in the most uncompromising circles, which were unheard of in earlier generations. Religious newspapers were first founded to counteract the ideas publicized by non-religious circles. As long as Jews did not read other newspapers, there was no need to publish a religious one. The same applies to today's need for schools that are able to equip young women for life in the wide world.

The same principle also applies to the range of subjects that should be studied by women. In the past, women were generally not introduced to those aspects of Torah study, such as abstract concepts, which did not relate to the actual performance of the *mitzvos*.[12] Today, women are commonly

---

12. For a start, there is a statement in the *Gemara* (*Sotah* 20a) which advises against teaching women the Oral Law. As to the conditions under which

exposed to the sophisticated demands of professional involvement in contemporary society (not to speak of the professional training that precedes it); they obviously need to prepare themselves for this by developing their thinking processes *within* the conceptual realm of the Torah and *within* the value system of the Torah.[13] This entails studying not only the practical application of the *mitzvos*, but also their conceptual underpinning.[14]

SHARING KNOWLEDGE

Women are characterized by warmth and a tendency to give. It is thus natural for women to share their newly-attained insights with others, beginning with the members of their families. The Book of *Psalms*[15] refers to a woman as *akeres habayis*, a term which can be understood to mean "the mainstay of the house." The woman determines the tone of the home environment: inspired by her own study, the encouragement she gives is crucial in motivating her husband and children to study further.

Moreover, the success of *chinuch* (education) depends on the development of a personal connection with the subject studied. This is stimulated by the love and positive approach

---

this counsel applies, see the closely-documented study by R. Pevsner mentioned above in footnote 7.

13. A definitive and practical shift in this direction began in the days of the Rebbe Rayatz and the *Chafetz Chayim* and their contemporaries, who applied the requirements of the Torah to the social situation already current in their day, by advocating the establishment of girls' schools with solid Torah content. (See also footnote 21 below.)

14. There is another positive corollary of these sociological changes. Since women often earn money independently, they should also take an increasing role in charitable activities, both by contributing a tenth (and preferably a fifth) of their income to deserving causes, and by inviting increasing numbers of guests to their homes.

15. 113:9.

generated by the teacher, and women have the natural gifts needed to build on this. Thus, in the typical situation, while a father contributes to a child's education primarily through testing his grasp of his school subjects, a mother discusses them with her child and focuses on the aspects which are relevant to his life. Furthermore, being more in daily contact with the child and more attuned to his day-to-day feelings, she is commonly better placed to communicate those educational messages in terms which her child can relate to.

A Cycle of Growth

By their very nature, such efforts at enlightening others rebound on the giver. When instructing adults to alert their children to the requirements of the *mitzvos*, the Sages[16] use the expression, *lehazhir*. Literally, this verb means "to warn" — but the Rebbe *Rayatz* points out[17] that it also shares a root with the word *zohar*, which means "radiance". In other words, through educating children, one's own knowledge is enhanced to a point at which the teacher or parent himself becomes radiant.

Here, then, we have a self-perpetuating cycle of growth. An increase in women's Torah knowledge should stimulate their efforts to educate others, and this, in turn, will upgrade their own knowledge.

---

16. *Rashi* on *Vayikra* 21:1, based on *Yevamos* 114a.
17. In the *maamar* beginning, *Zeh HaYom Asah HaShem*, 5708, end of sec. 2. See *Lessons In Tanya* (Kehot; N.Y., 1987), Vol. I, pp. 26-27, for the Alter Rebbe's exposition of the teaching of the Sages (*Temurah* 16a) on *Mishlei* 29:13: "G-d enlightens the eyes of them both."

A FORETASTE OF THE MESSIANIC AGE

The Sages teach[18] that on Friday, before the actual arrival of *Shabbos*, it is a *mitzvah* to taste the delicacies to be served on that day. At present, in the era directly before the coming of the *Mashiach*, on the very eve of[19] "the day which is entirely *Shabbos*," it is a *mitzvah* to enjoy a foretaste of the revelations of that age. The Messianic age will be characterized by an abundance of knowledge:[20] "The occupation of the entire world will be solely to know G-d. The Jews will therefore be great sages and know the hidden matters." Hence, in eager anticipation of that time, the present age should also be characterized by an ever-widening availability of knowledge.[21]

AN URGENT NATIONAL PRIORITY

Ultimately, the collective endeavors of Jewish women around the world to broaden and deepen their Torah learning, and to share it with others, will bring about a long-awaited change in the world at large. Our Sages remind us that[22] "In the merit of the righteous women [of that generation], our forefathers were redeemed from Egypt." In the same way, the merit of today's women, who are raising and educating a generation of children prepared to greet

---

18. The Alter Rebbe's *Shulchan Aruch* 250:8.
19. *Tamid* 7:4.
20. *Mishneh Torah, Hilchos Melachim* 12:5.
21. In this spirit, the Rebbe Rayatz took the initiative — a revolutionary step for his era — of writing to several of the prominent communal leaders of his generation, advocating the formal Torah education of women. (See *Sefer HaSichos 5750* [1990], p. 539, and footnotes there.) Though his approach was not accepted by them all, his efforts and example helped to popularize it among all sectors of the Jewish people. Over and above the various socio-economic reasons for such a change, it should be perceived as one of the steps which both heralds and hastens the coming of the Redemption.
22. *Sotah* 11b.

Mashiach, will prepare the world for the age when[23] "the world will be filled with the knowledge of G-d as the waters cover the ocean bed."

Seen in this light, for women today to study Torah in depth is not merely a right or a privilege, but an urgent national priority.

---

23. *Yeshayahu* 11:9, quoted by *Rambam* as the culminating thought of his *Mishneh Torah*.

Actions Speak Louder

THREE PIVOTAL MITZVOS

Our[1] Sages teach[2] that 613 *mitzvos* were given to the Jewish people at Mount Sinai. "David... condensed them into eleven, as it is written,[3] 'He who walks uprightly and acts justly, and who speaks the truth in his heart....' Yeshayahu... condensed them into six, as it is written,[4] 'He who walks righteously... and shuts his eyes from seeing evil.' Michah... condensed them into three, as it is written,[5] 'To act justly, to love kindness, and to walk humbly with your G-d.' Chavakuk... condensed them into one, as it is written,[6] 'A righteous man lives by his faith.'"

Obviously enough, these prophets did not reduce the number of *mitzvos*. Rather, they highlighted the dominant

---

1. The above essay is adapted from talks of the Rebbe as published in *Likkutei Sichos*: Vol. XIII, pp. 256ff., 259ff., 274ff., 280ff., 295ff.; Vol. XVIII, p. 157; Vol. XX, p. 227; Vol. XXIX, p. 498ff. See also *Sefer HaSichos 5751*, p. 566ff.; *sichos* of 26 Sivan, 5729.
2. *Makkos* 23b.
3. *Tehillim* 15:2.
4. *Yeshayahu* 33:15.
5. *Michah* 6:8.
6. *Chavakuk* 2:4.

thrusts which, when internalized, upgrade one's observance of *all* the commandments.[7]

A similar concept applies to the three fundamental *mitzvos* which our Sages[8] associate with Jewish women: (a) *challah* — the separation for the *Kohen* of a portion of the dough being prepared for baking, and by extension,[9] the preparation of kosher food in its entirety; (b) *niddah* — the observance of the Torah's guidelines for maintaining the purity of marital life; and (c) *hadlakas haner* — the lighting of candles to usher the *Shabbos* and festivals into our homes. As will soon be seen, their dominant thrusts span the entire gamut of commandments that women observe.

The name Chanah (חנה) serves as an acronym for the Hebrew names of these three *mitzvos* (חלה, נדה, הדלקת הנר), for the prophetess Chanah serves as a paradigm for Jewish women.[10] The Biblical narrative as expounded in the *Midrashim* underscores her unique contributions as a wife and as a mother, and accentuates her activities beyond her household through which she inspired the Jewish people as a whole. These three *mitzvos* lead to precisely the same goals: They help a woman to weave the physical and spiritual fabric of her home, to forge a link to posterity, and to transform her home into a lantern that will illuminate its environment.

When rearranged, the letters of the name Chanah also form the word *hachen* (החן), which means "grace", and thus

---

7. Cf. *Likkutei Sichos*, Vol. XVIII, p. 157, *et al.*

8. *Talmud Yerushalmi, Shabbos* 2:6; *Tanchuma,* beg. of *Parshas Noach; Bereishis Rabbah,* end of sec. 17; *Or HaTorah, Parshas Shlach,* p. 535ff.; *Toras Shmuel 5627,* pp. 309ff. & 315ff.

9. Bread, for example, as man's staple food, sometimes signifies an entire meal (as in *I Melachim* 5:2 and *II Melachim* 25:29), or, in a broader sense, all our material needs.

10. *I Shmuel,* chs. 1-2. The source for the above-quoted acronym is *Megaleh Amukos* on the Torah, *Parshas Shlach, s.v. Gimmel mitzvos,* sec. 17:4, citing the author of *Haggahos Maimuni.*

points to the quality which characterizes a woman's observance of these *mitzvos*. Moreover, this association also implies that the observance of these *mitzvos* amplifies the gentle
grace which is an innate gift of women.

UPLIFTING PHYSICALITY

In particular, each of these *mitzvos* contributes a lesson of
its own. The observance of the commandment of *challah*
(and, by extension, maintaining a *kosher* diet) shows the
uniqueness of the Torah lifestyle: the fusion between the
spiritual and the material realms that it encourages. For the
Torah's spiritual truth was never intended to be confined to
some sphere that wafts above our physical reality; it is meant
to permeate the realm of physical experience. Even eating,
drinking, and other physical activities in which Jews appear
to resemble the other nations, are to be carried out in a
manner which expresses the connection we share with G-d.

To see how this ideal is translated into actuality, we need
only look at the *mitzvah* of *challah*. When one's dough has
been kneaded, part of it is set aside, distinguished as holy,
and given to a priest. This gift is not a sacrifice to be burnt
on the altar: it is eaten. The pattern thus established, the
separation and elevation of materiality, should be extended
to all aspects of our interaction with our material environment. First, we must set aside and distinguish a certain portion — indeed, the choicest portion — of our mundane
endeavors. By elevating this sample, and accentuating its
spiritual dimension, we simultaneously elevate the entire
remaining range of these endeavors.

This insight sheds light on a perplexing Talmudic pas-
sage. Our Sages ask,[11] "How does a woman help a man?" —

---

11. *Yevamos* 63a.

and they answer with rhetorical questions: "If a man brings home wheat does he chew it? If [he brings home] flax does he wear it? If so, does she not bring light to his eyes and put him on his feet?"

What lies at the heart of this seemingly simplistic summary of a woman's wifely functions? Is its focus on mere materiality?

These questions can be resolved by examining the ultimate source for all male-female relationships: the bond between G-d and the Jewish people which our Sages compare to a marriage link.

The home for this ultimate couple is our world, which G-d created with the intent that it serve as His dwelling. Yet though He created the raw materials for its construction, He delegated to the Jewish people — His wife, as it were — the responsibility of processing these raw materials, and infusing them with spiritual purpose.

In microcosm, this is the task performed by every Jewish woman in her homemaking efforts. And this affects the macrocosm, the universe — for ordinary activities, such as processing wheat and flax into useful artifacts, are the very stuff with which G-d's ultimate desire is fulfilled.

KASHRUS: YOU ARE WHAT YOU EAT

Executing this task has far-reaching benefits. On the most obvious level, a woman is responsible for the physical health and well-being of those who depend on her judgment. Beyond that, since the food one eats is quite literally transformed into one's own flesh and blood,[12] there is a responsibility for the effects of this food on the family's tendencies and character traits. If, for example, a person eats an animal

---

12. Cf. *Tanya*, ch. 8.

of prey, then while its flesh is being digested in his stomach, its tendency to cruelty percolates imperceptibly through to his soul.[13] Finally, over and above the effects of a person's eating habits on his *middos*, there is a comparable effect on his mode of thinking:[14] coarse and gross food predisposes the mind to coarseness and grossness, whereas refined food makes its perception clearer and more refined.[15]

Though these concepts are also relevant to men, the responsibility in this area is primarily a woman's: the choices as to her household's diet are mainly hers.

FAMILY PURITY: BUILDING ETERNITY

The inextricable bond between material and spiritual is further tightened by the next of the three *mitzvos* — observance of the laws of *niddah*, and adherence to the Torah's directives concerning family life. Here, too, a basic physical activity[16] draws down the highest spiritual energies: it is

---

13. See *Ramban* (cited by Rabbeinu Bachaye) on *Vayikra* 11:13; *Akeidah*, Abarbanel, and others, *loc. cit.*; *Ramban* on *Devarim* 14:3; R. Moshe Isserles, *Yoreh Deah*, end of sec. 1:7; and elsewhere.

As the Rebbe observes (in *Likkutei Sichos*, Vol. III, p. 984ff., and footnotes there), this insight enables us to understand why a nursing mother who has eaten forbidden food, even when permitted to do so because her life was endangered, should refrain from nursing her child. (See *Taz (Turei Zahav)* and *Shach (Sifsei Kohen)* in *Shulchan Aruch, Yoreh Deah*, end of sec. 81.) For although eating this food was in fact halachically permitted, the nature of the food and the spiritual blemish which it imparts to her infant remain unchanged. (Cf. *Rambam, Hilchos Shabbos*, beg. of ch. 2.)

14. Cf. *Keser Shem Tov*, sec. 381 (also sec. 186), citing the writings of the *Rambam*.

15. See, e.g., *Shelah, Shaar HaOsiyos*, sec. 85b.

16. The Rebbe notes that these three *mitzvos* all share a significant characteristic: they all deal with basic needs and activities that are shared by all of humanity — the provision of light, the preparation of food, and the maintenance of family life. What is required of a Jew is that he transform these human activities into *Jewish* activities. See *Likkutei Sichos*, Vol. XX, p. 227.

through conception that the *Ein Sof*, G-d's infinity, is revealed.[17]

The Torah's guidelines enhance the relationship between a woman and her husband and endow it with purity. Above all, these guidelines nurture eternity, since they prepare for the conception of children in holiness.

For a soul to function in all its pristine refinement and purity even while enclothed in a body, it needs to be summoned down to this world in conditions of refinement and purity. In other words, the newborn body which is to host it for a lifetime needs to be conceived according to the principles that govern family purity, *taharas hamishpachah*. This prior condition affects the "garments" of the soul,[18] i.e., the means by which the soul finds expression in the body.[19]

This *mitzvah*, too, is also relevant to men; indeed, the very name "family purity" is a reminder that this *mitzvah* affects the entire family. Nevertheless, the responsibility for its observance centers on women. This primary responsibility finds explicit expression in Torah law,[20] which grants a woman unique authority to define the state of ritual purity that determines the periodic resumption of relations.

SHABBOS CANDLES: DISPELLING GLOOM

One of the special gifts of women is — generating light. This is the contribution of the third *mitzvah*, the lighting of

17. See the *maamar* beginning *Kol HaNeheneh 5652*; see also *Likkutei Torah, Shir HaShirim*, p. 40a.
18. It also affects the physical health of the body; see: *Sefer HaSichos 5700*, p. 19ff.; *Likkutei Dibburim* (in English translation: Kehot, N.Y.), Vol. III, ch. 21, sec. 25; and Vol. IV, in the first Appendix to ch. 30. See also the sources enumerated in the next footnote.
19. *Zohar* II, 3b; cf. *Tanchuma*, beginning of *Parshas Metzora*; *Vayikra Rabbah* 15:5; *Ramban* on *Vayikra* 18:19; *Tanya*, end of ch. 2; and elsewhere.
20. See *Shulchan Aruch, Yoreh Deah*, ch. 185:1.

candles in honor of *Shabbos* and the festivals.[21] Just as in a physical sense, a candle reveals the otherwise-unseen contents of a room, so, too, in a spiritual sense, the *Shabbos* candles of Jewish women and girls reveal the unseen and intangible G-dly energy which permeates our existence.

The spiritual light generated by a woman's *Shabbos* candles illuminates the home, not only on *Shabbos*, but also during the weekdays that follow. In this vein, the *Midrash*[22] tells us that the *Shabbos* lamps kindled by Sarah Imeinu, our matriarch Sarah, continued to burn for an entire week. Moreover, this miracle repeated itself whenever her daughter-in-law, Rivkah Imeinu, lit candles. And, less visibly, the same miracle occurs whenever a Jewish woman or girl lights her *Shabbos* candles.

It will be noted that Rivkah Imeinu lit her candles before marriage. From her example we see what a three-year-old[23] Jewish girl can do: she can kindle lamps which will radiate light for an entire week.

Every little Jewish girl who is old enough to appreciate the significance of what she is doing can mirror that light — by lighting candles every Friday, and before every festival. The more candles lit around the world, the more light. For even[24] "a little light dispels a great deal of darkness." And the increase in the spiritual darkness that beclouds the world

---

21. The *farbrengen* on this subject on *Shabbos Parshas Chayei Sarah*, 5735 [1974] (see *Likkutei Sichos*, Vol. XV, p. 163-173) was originally adapted and published as an essay entitled "The *Shabbos* Lights" by Sichos In English.

22. *Bereishis Rabbah* (and *Rashi*) commenting on *Bereishis* 24:67. These sources also allude to the other two *mitzvos* of which we have spoken, for in the case of both Sarah and Rivkah, "there was always a blessing in the dough" (an allusion to the *mitzvah* of *challah*), and "a cloud hovered over the tent" (an allusion to *taharas hamishpachah*, for the cloud distinguished this dwelling's holiness).

23. *Rashi* on *Bereishis* 25:20.

24. *Tzeidah LaDerech*, sec. 12.

today has to be met by an increase in spiritual light — by[25] "a *mitzvah* [which] is a candle and by the Torah [which] is light," and, in a most literal sense, by the *mitzvah*-candles lit every Friday night.

Though this commandment, too, obligates men as well as women, it has been entrusted to those in whose hands its observance is most powerful. To refer back to the *Midrash* mentioned above: Although Abraham lit *Shabbos* candles after Sarah's death, they did not burn throughout the week. That enduring achievement was the prerogative of Sarah, representing all Jewish women, and of Rivkah, representing all Jewish girls.

LIGHTING THE ROAD FOR MASHIACH

We have G-d's longstanding promise:[26] "If you cherish the lights of *Shabbos*, I will show you the lights of Zion." *Shabbos* is a foretaste of[27] "the Day which is entirely *Shabbos*, and repose for life everlasting," i.e., the World to Come. Kindling *Shabbos* candles anticipates — and precipitates — the enlightenment of that future era.

Similarly, the purifying waters of *taharas hamishpachah* clear a path for the Redemption. For, as our Sages explain, the coming of the Redemption is dependent on the birth of more and more children.[28] In that age, moreover, we will merit the fulfillment of the prophecies,[29] "I will sprinkle upon

25. *Mishlei* 6:23.
26. *Yalkut Shimoni, Parshas Behaalos'cha*, sec. 719.
27. *Tamid* 7:4.
28. *Yevamos* 62b; see also the above essays entitled "Family Planning" and "Three Mothers."
29. *Yechezkel* 36:25.

you purifying waters and you will become pure," and[30] "I will remove the spirit of impurity from the earth."

The *mitzvah* of kosher food is also connected with the era of which it is written,[31] "I will destroy dangerous animals within the land"; beasts of prey will cease to exist. Moreover, G-d will prepare a feast for the righteous, and their partaking of it will depend on newly-revealed insights into the laws of *kashrus*.[32]

Ultimately, sprouting out of all the day-by-day physical/spiritual wedding preparations in the home of G-d's eager and industrious "bride", the marriage bond between G-d and the Jewish people will blossom into consummation. In that age we will merit the fulfillment of the prophecy,[33] "I will greatly rejoice in G-d... for He has clothed me with the garments of salvation..., as a bridegroom garbs himself in priestlike apparel, and as a bride adorns herself with jewels."

30. *Zechariah* 13:2.
31. *Vayikra* 26:6.
32. *Vayikra Rabbah* 13:3.
33. *Yeshayahu* 61:10.

A Lifetime Renewed

DESCENT FOR THE SAKE OF ASCENT

The[1] Biblical simile,[2] "As a rose among the thorns," refers to the soul as it descends into this material world; on a larger scale, it also refers to the existence of the Jewish people within exile. For both the soul and the Jewish people, this involves a formidable descent, a descent fraught with danger. At times, the path of life appears to be obstructed by brambles: events sometimes occur which our limited human intellect cannot comprehend. Paradoxically, however, it is through this very process of descent that both the soul and the Jewish people as a whole ultimately climb to their most complete level of perfection.

1. The above essay first appeared after the *farbrengen* of *Shabbos Parshas Bo,* 5752 [1992], which took place four days before *Yud* Shvat — the anniversary of the passing in 5710 [1950] of the Rebbe Rayatz, the saintly Rabbi Yosef Yitzchak Schneersohn נ"ע. On this occasion, the Rebbe spoke of the ultimate purpose for which souls descend to this world, which is one of the dominant themes of the Previous Rebbe's farewell *maamar,* entitled *Basi LeGani* (English translation: Kehot; N.Y., 1990), and related it in particular to the souls of women.

2. *Shir HaShirim* 2:2, and commentaries there.

This is not to imply, heaven forbid, that the world is in itself evil. Quite the contrary:[3] "I have come into My garden" is a metaphor that describes the return of the Divine Presence to this world. This indicates that the world is G-d's own garden, a place which grants Him pleasure and satisfaction. Though we are often unable to perceive this positive quality, the Jewish people have been charged with a task and a mission: Holding aloft[4] "the lamp of a *mitzvah* and the light of the Torah," they illuminate the world and reveal the good which is concealed within it.

WOMEN AS LUMINARIES

In particular, this quality is manifest in those *mitzvos* that are associated with producing actual light; for example, the kindling of *Shabbos* candles. The visible light which they generate reflects how every *mitzvah*, and in a wider sense, every positive activity a Jew undertakes, brightens the G-dly light within the world. The *mitzvah* of lighting the *Shabbos* candles has been entrusted to Jewish women;[5] it is they who draw G-dly light into every Jewish home, and suffuse it with the inimitable *Shabbos* atmosphere of tranquil joy and spiritual enlightenment.

On a cosmic scale, the world has been described as G-d's dwelling[6] — His home, as it were, and the Jewish people have been described as His bride.[7] Developing these analogies: Just as the *Shabbos* candles are lit before the actual

---

3. *Op. cit.* 5:1. This verse is the subject of the above-mentioned *maamar* entitled *Basi LeGani*.
4. *Mishlei* 6:23. On the analogy of a lamp for *mitzvos*, see footnote 19 to the above essay entitled, "A Partner in the Dynamic of Creation."
5. *Rambam, Mishneh Torah, Hilchos Shabbos* 5:3; the Alter Rebbe's *Shulchan Aruch* 263:5.
6. *Midrash Tanchuma, Parshas Naso*, sec. 7; *Tanya*, chs. 33, 36.
7. E.g., *Yeshayahu* 62:5.

commencement of the *Shabbos*, our present performance of *mitzvos* in exile kindles the light that will illuminate the world in[8] "the Day which is entirely *Shabbos*, and repose for life everlasting" — the Era of the Redemption. This connection also highlights the role of Jewish women, for the prophecies associated with that age[9] point out the superior qualities which Jewish women possess.

ETERNAL LIFE IN THIS WORLD

The eternality which will characterize the Era of the Redemption is likewise reflected in every individual Jewish soul. This applies not only to the soul as it exists in the spiritual realms, where it enjoys eternal life in the radiance of the Divine Presence,[10] but also to the time it spends in our physical world.

In this spirit, our Sages state in regard to the Patriarch Jacob,[11] "Our father Yaakov did not die: just as his descendants are alive, so too is He alive." The same is true of each of Yaakov Avinu's descendants, the Jewish men and women of all subsequent generations. When a person's children continue the positive activities which characterized his own lifetime, then even after that person's passing, he or she is still alive. For that life has activated a dynamic which continues to produce positive changes in the world in the generations to come. And there is also a reciprocal effect: the positive activities performed by one's children can compensate for any time by which a person's life may have been cut short. Even when a mother is now in the World of Truth, the daughters whom she brought up, and her sons likewise,

---

8.   *Tamid* 7:4.
9.   Cf. *Yirmeyahu* 31:21, as interpreted in the teachings of *Chassidus*.
10. Cf. *Rambam, Mishneh Torah, Hilchos Teshuvah*, ch. 8.
11. *Taanis* 5b.

can replenish the divine service which is now lacking, and which ordinarily would have been completed by her.[12]

THE PINNACLE OF OUR NATIONAL HISTORY

The eternality of the Jewish soul within the context of our material world will be fully expressed in the Era of the Redemption, when the souls of all the Jews of all generations will be resurrected.[13] Here too the analogy of a wedding can be used to describe the unification of the body and the soul.

The ultimate Redemption of our people and of the world at large is not a remote promise. On the contrary, the Jews of our generation have been granted complete atonement and are now at the highest pinnacle ever of our national history. All the divine service necessary to bring about the Redemption has been completed. All that is needed is that we open our eyes and perceive that the Redemption is indeed a reality.

Our Sages state[14] that the *tzadikkim* of all past generations will arise in the early stages of the Redemption, before the resurrection of our people as a whole. Surely, this applies to the Previous Rebbe, the leader of our generation. He never perceived himself as a private individual and dedicated him-

---

12. In addition to the above explicit statement, this *farbrengen* included a mystical exposition of a liturgical phrase in which the people of Israel are referred to poetically as a rose, and a mention of the fact that the Sages extol the *Kohanim* for the vigor with which they traditionally carry out their priestly duties. Though personal allusions of this kind are not common, these phrases collectively were an apparent reference to *Rebbitzin* Reizel (Rose) Gutnick ע״ה, the wife of a *Kohen* and the mother of a family of *Kohanim* — an exemplary chassidic wife and mother who lost her life in a traffic accident two days before the above address. (Publisher's Note.)
13. Cf. *Sanhedrin* 10:1.
14. *Zohar* I, 140a.

self totally to the welfare of his people.[15] It can thus be readily understood that he will share this privilege too (just as throughout his lifetime he always shared his insights) with all the members of his generation,[16] particularly with those who dedicated themselves to disseminating his teachings and furthering the outreach activity which he inspired. And when that time comes, we will all proceed together — to *Eretz Yisrael*, to Jerusalem, and to the *Beis HaMikdash*, where the *Kohanim* will offer sacrifices celebrating[17] "our redemption and the deliverance of our souls."

---

15. This concept was once expressed by his daughter, the *Rebbitzin* Chayah Mushka, of blessed memory, in these words: "Not only the Rebbe's library, but also the Rebbe himself belongs to the chassidim."

16. Ch. 11 of *Basi LeGani* describes a king confronted by a formidable and ultimate battle. In order to secure victory he will even distribute the "hidden and sealed treasures,... the precious resources that have been accumulated over the generations," to his rank-and-file soldiers.

   The Rebbe has commented that these words aptly describe the activities of their author, the Previous Rebbe. He fought fiercely to overcome the challenges brought about by the darkness of *galus*. He risked (and sacrificed) his own life and revealed the ancient treasures of the kingdom — the deepest secrets of the Torah. These were then entrusted to the rank-and-file soldiers; i.e., they were expressed in a manner that could be understood and appreciated by all.

17. From the *Haggadah* of Pesach.

aliyah (עליה; pl., *aliyos*; lit., "ascent"): the honor of being called upon in synagogue to ascend to the dais for the public Reading of the Torah

Beis HaMikdash (בית המקדש): the (First or Second) Temple in Jerusalem

Chabad (חב״ד; acronym formed by the initial letters of the Heb. words *chochmah*, *binah* and *daas*): (a) the branch of the chassidic movement (see **Chassidus*) whose roots are in an intellectual approach to the service of G-d, and which was founded by R. Shneur Zalman of Liadi, the Alter Rebbe; a synonym for *Chabad* in this sense is **Lubavitch*, the name of the township where the movement flourished 1813-1915; (b) the philosophy of this school of Chassidism

challah (חלה): (a) in the time of the **Beis HaMikdash*, a mandatory contribution of dough for the **Kohen*; (b) a usually braided loaf (pl., *challos*) baked in honor of **Shabbos*

Chassidus (חסידות): Chassidism, i.e., (a) the movement within Orthodox Judaism founded in the eighteenth century by R. Yisrael, the Baal Shem Tov, and stressing: emotional involvement in prayer; service of G-d through the material universe; the primacy of wholehearted earnestness in divine service; the mystical in addition to the legalistic dimension of Judaism; the power of joy, and of music; the love to be shown to *every* fellow Jew, unconditionally; and the mutual physical and moral responsibility of the members of the informal chassidic brotherhood, each chassid having cultivated a spiritual attachment to their saintly and charismatic leader, the *Rebbe; (b) the philosophy and literature of this movement; see also *Chabad

Chumash (חומש): the Five Books of Moses (the Pentateuch)

Ein Sof (אין סוף): the Infinite One

Eretz Yisrael (ארץ ישראל): the Land of Israel

farbrengen (פארברענגען): a chassidic gathering addressed by the Rebbe

hadlakas haner (הדלקת הנר): the lighting of candles [in honor of *Shabbos* or *Yom-Tov*]

Halachah (הלכה): Torah law

Kabbalah (קבלה; lit., "received tradition"): the body of classical Jewish mystical teachings

kashrus (כשרות): the state of being kosher, i.e., ritually valid or fit for use

Kohen (כהן; pl., *Kohanim*): "priest"; i.e., a descendant of Aharon

kuntreis (קונטרס): booklet

lekach (לעקעך; Yid.): sweet cake

Lubavitch (lit., "town of love"; Rus.): townlet in White Russia which from 1813-1915 was the center of *Chabad *Chassidism, and whose name has remained a synonym for it

Mashiach (משיח; lit., "the anointed one"): Messiah

Megillah (מגילה; pl., *megillos*): a scroll, esp. the Scroll of *Esther* which is publicly read on *Purim

Midrash (מדרש): one of the classical collections of the Sages' homiletical teachings on the Torah, on the non-literal level of *derush*

minyan (מנין): (a) quorum of at least ten adult males assembled for prayer or other *mitzvah*; (b) place of public prayer; *shul*

Mishkan (משכן): the Tabernacle, i.e., the temporary Sanctuary in the wilderness; see *Shmos* 25ff.

mitzvah (מצוה; pl., *mitzvos*): a religious obligation; one of the 613 Commandments

Motzaei [Shabbos, etc.] (מוצאי [שבת]): evening on which [a *Shabbos* or *Yom-Tov*] ends

parshah (פרשה; pl., *parshiyos*): portion of the Torah read publicly each week

Parshas... (פרשת...): the *Parshah* of [a certain *Shabbos* or festive occasion]

pnimiyus (פנימיות): the innermost, mystical dimension [of the Torah]

Purim (פורים; lit., "lots"): one-day festival falling on 14 Adar and commemorating the miraculous salvation of the Jews of the Persian Empire in the 4th cent. B.C.E.

pushke (פושקע; Yid.): box [for charity]

Rebbe (common Yid. pronunciation of רבי, "my teacher [or master]"): *tzaddik* who serves as spiritual guide to a following of *chassidim*

Rebbitzin (רעביצין; Yid.): wife of a *rav* or Rebbe

Rosh HaShanah (ראש השנה; lit., "head of the year"): the New Year festival, falling on 1 and 2 Tishrei

Sefirah (ספירה; pl., *Sefiros*): divine attributes or emanations which are manifested in each of the Four Worlds, and are the source of the ten corresponding faculties (*kochos*) of the soul

Shechinah (שכינה): the Divine Presence

Shabbos (שבת): the Sabbath

Siddur (סדור; lit., "order [of prayers]"): prayer book

Sukkos (סוכות; lit., "Booths"): seven-day festival beginning on 15 Tishrei, taking its name from the temporary dwelling in which one lives during this period, and marked also by the *mitzvah* of Four Species

taharas hamishpachah (טהרת המשפחה): the marital laws that safeguard a family's purity and integrity

Talmud (תלמוד): the basic compendium of Jewish law, thought, and Biblical commentary; its tractates mainly comprise the discussions collectively known as the *Gemara*, which elucidate the germinal statements of law (*mishnayos*) collectively known as the *Mishnah*; when unspecified refers to the *Talmud Bavli*, the edition developed in Babylonia, and edited at end of the fifth century C.E.; the *Talmud Yerushalmi* is the edition compiled in *Eretz Yisrael* at end of the fourth century C.E.

Tanach (תנ"ך): acronym for Torah (i.e., the Five Books of Moses), *Nevi'im* (Prophets), and *Kesuvim* (the Holy Writings; i.e., the Hagiographa)

Tanya (תניא): the Alter Rebbe's basic exposition of *Chabad *Chassidus; "*Tanya*" is the initial word of the book, which is also called *Likkutei Amarim* ("Collected Discourses") and *Sefer shel Beinonim* ("The Book of the Intermediates")

tefillin (תפילין): small black leather cubes containing parchment scrolls inscribed with *Shema Yisrael* and other Biblical passages, bound to the arm and forehead and worn by men at weekday morning prayers

tzaddik (צדיק; pl., *tzaddikim*): (a) completely righteous individual; (b) Rebbe

tzedakah (צדקה): charity

tzniyus (צניעות): modesty

yahrzeit (יאהרצייט; Yid.): the anniversary of an individual's passing

yechidus (יחידות): private interview (rather: a meeting of souls) at which a chassid seeks guidance and enlightenment from his Rebbe

Yiddishkeit (ייִדישקייט; lit., "Jewishness"; Yid.): the Torah way of life

Yom-Tov (יום-טוב): a festival

zemiros (זמירות): the hymns sung at the *Shabbos* and *Yom-Tov* table

Zohar (זהר; lit., "radiance"): classical work containing the mystical teachings of the *Kabbalah*

Hebrew/English Names of Biblical Books Cited

Transliteration of Hebrew Name	English Equivalent
Bamidbar	Numbers
Bereishis	Genesis
Chavakuk	Habakkuk
Devarim	Deuteronomy
Divrei HaYamim	Chronicles
Melachim	Kings
Michah	Micah
Mishlei	Proverbs
Shir HaShirim	Song of Songs
Shmos	Exodus
Shmuel	Samuel
Tehillim	Psalms
Vayikra	Leviticus
Yechezkel	Ezekiel
Yeshayahu	Isaiah
Yirmeyahu	Jeremiah
Zechariah	Zachariah

Dedicated to the Lubavitcher Rebbe

*whose teachings and example are a
never-ending source of life for all mankind.
May we continue in his paths, and complete
the mission with which he has charged us:
to make the world conscious of the imminent
Redemption and to prepare an environment
in which this ideal can be realized.*

& In Memory of

Behira bas Yaakov ע״ה Kaiser

Rivka bas Avraham Yaakov ע״ה Kimball

Gittel bas Yosef ע״ה Klein

Chaya bas Moshe ע״ה Stien

Dedicated by

Tzivia Devorah שתחי׳ bas Yissacher ע״ה Kimball

Chaya שתחי׳ bas Reuven Dovid שיחי׳ Kimball